Creative
Curriculum
Leadership

This book is dedicated to
R. Murray Thomas—
scholar, mentor, and friend

Second Edition

Creative
Curriculum
Leadership

Inspiring and Empowering
Your School Community

Dale L. Brubaker

CORWIN PRESS
A Sage Publications Company
Thousand Oaks, California

For information:

Corwin Press
A Sage Publications Company
2455 Teller Road
Thousand Oaks, California 91320
www.corwinpress.com

Sage Publications Ltd.
1 Oliver's Yard
55 City Road
London EC1Y 1SP
United Kingdom

Sage Publications India Pvt. Ltd.
B-42, Panchsheel Enclave
Post Box 4109
New Delhi 110 017 India

Printed in the United States of America

Library of Congress Cataloging-in-Publication Data

Brubaker, Dale L.
Creative curriculum leadership : inspiring and empowering your school community / by Dale L. Brubaker.—2nd ed.
        p. cm.
Includes bibliographical references and index.
ISBN 0-7619-3993-8 (Cloth)—ISBN 0-7619-3994-6 (Paper)
    1. Curriculum planning—United States. 2. Curriculum change—United States. 3. Educational leadership—United States. I. Title.
LB2806.15.B78 2004
375'.001--dc22

                                            2003022998

03   04   05   06   07   10   9   8   7   6   5   4   3   2   1

Acquisitions Editor:	Kylee M. Liegl
Editorial Assistant:	Jaime L. Cuvier
Production Editor:	Julia Parnell
Copy Editor:	Elizabeth Budd
Typesetter:	C&M Digitals (P) Ltd.
Proofreader:	Taryn Bigelow
Indexer:	Jean Casalegno
Cover Designer:	Michael Dubowe
Graphic Designer:	Lisa Miller

Contents

Foreword to the Second Edition   v
 R. Murray Thomas
Foreword to the First Edition   ix
 Louis J. Rubin
Preface   xiii

About the Author   xxiii

Prologue: A Cautionary Tale   xxv

Part I. The Meaning of Curriculum   1

1. Introduction: Developing One's Own Curriculum   3

2. Defining Inner and Outer Curriculum   13

**Part II. Education as Vocation: How a "Sense of
 Calling" Influences Curriculum Development**   29

3. Learning From Your Professional Autobiography   33

4. Looking Forward to Work:
 The Power of Wanting to Be There   49

5. Keeping the Fire in Your Vocation   57

**Part III. Curriculum Development Can Make
 a Difference**   67

6. Creative Curriculum Leadership in Practice   71

7. Civility in Leadership: The Ultimate Difference   105

8. Creating Learning Communities   127

9. Teacher Leaders   149

Appendices   175

References   193

Index   197

Foreword to the Second Edition

The remarkable popularity of the first edition of *Creative Curriculum Leadership* seems to have resulted from a variety of novel attractions. Not only are those attractions retained in this new edition of the book, but new ones have been added as well.

Among the innovations retained from the first edition, two that I find particularly engaging are (a) Professor Brubaker's definition of *inner curriculum* and (b) the case descriptions at the ends of chapters that challenge readers to choose among alternative reactions to the cases and to analyze the rationales offered in support of each alternative.

DEFINING CURRICULUM

Over the years, people have assigned different meanings to the term *curriculum*. In its most common meaning, *curriculum* refers to the printed *course of study* that describes the knowledge and skills learners are expected to acquire at different grade levels. Some educators expand this definition to include the textbooks, worksheets, videotapes, and other learning materials whose contents students are urged to master.

Another meaning for curriculum is limited to what the teacher actually teaches. This is the *taught curriculum*. The notion of a taught curriculum derives from the fact that teachers do not precisely reproduce the course of study during their instruction. Instead, they emphasize some topics more than others and add their own interpretations. They embellish, repeat, and skip topics. They introduce skills and knowledge beyond those in the course of study.

A third meaning is the *experienced curriculum,* in reference to what each student actually learns. Students differ from each other in their native abilities, background knowledge, interests, anxieties that distract them from their lessons, and more. Consequently, no two students experience classroom instruction in precisely the same way. Each acquires something different from the instruction.

A fourth definition is featured in Professor Brubaker's *Creative Curriculum Leadership.* It's an extension of the experienced curriculum, an extension that focuses on the interaction of teacher and students. He calls it the *inner curriculum,* meaning that "what each person experiences as learning settings are cooperatively created." His comparisons throughout the book between the *outer curriculum* (course of study) and the *inner curriculum* lend this volume a unique character not found in traditional analyses of curriculum.

CASE ANALYSES

The final pages of each chapter in *Creative Curriculum Leadership* describe one or more real-life cases bearing on the chapter's key concepts. Each case closes with alternative reactions that readers might express about the issues involved, along with rationales in support of each alternative. As I read the cases, I found myself frequently saying, "Hey, wait a minute. How about . . .?" And then I would propose an addition to an alternative, or I would rework the interpretation and wonder why the author had not included my options. It was then I recognized that, with his cases, Professor Brubaker has cleverly provoked me into engaging in the active "inner curriculum" development that his book is all about. Throughout the volume he urges readers to consider their own perspectives on life and to recognize how each individual's worldview or "inner curriculum" affects what is taught and what is learned in schools. The cases at the close of each chapter immediately lure readers into recognizing that "what each person experiences as learning settings [in this instance, reading the book] are cooperatively created."

THE NEW EDITION'S ADDED FEATURES

The appeal of *Creative Curriculum Leadership*'s first edition is enhanced by additions to this new version, particularly Chapters 8 and 9 in which the author focuses on ways of developing leadership communities and on roles for teachers in curriculum leadership.

The opportunity for readers to fashion their own "inner curriculum" is further promoted in this edition by the activities in the six new appendices at the end of the book.

—R. Murray Thomas

Foreword to the First Edition

C reative Curriculum Leadership is a unique and useful addition to the curriculum literature. The book deals with the process dimensions of curriculum development through the prism of creative imagination and self-expression. The major underlying theme is that personal growth and professional development are symbiotic functions, which mutually nurture one another.

Among other things, the volume provides a vivid portrait of the ways in which creative inspiration and idealism can order and direct a vision of learning. In clear, concise, easily grasped arguments, the chapters demonstrate how each of us can use our talents and enterprise to improve the human lot. The infrastructure of the text is based on self-understanding, evolution, sensitivity to human settings, and the sequential cultivation of capacity and capability.

Philosophers have long posited that proper human action ought rightly to vary according to circumstance and situation. Because the motives underlying behavior are individually determined, psychologists fault the efforts of social scientists to devise a general theory of human action. As we engage in life, we not only make private moral determinations, but also tend to base our tactics on the conditions that prevail. So it is, seemingly, in schooling. There is no way to avoid either the benefits or the liabilities of free human action. Clearly, leaders should enable teachers to deepen their perceptions, increase their awareness, perfect their skills, and sharpen their sense of purpose. All of these, however, should not constitute a universal prescription. Just as the physician must qualify the

xii   Creative Curriculum Leadership

use of a drug, even within the range of standard practice, because it may not be appropriate in a particular situation, so must we make allowances for exceptions to standard practice in curriculum.

The downfall of much of the recent reform has, in large measure, been a consequence of faulty innovative process. Lesson plans, courses of study, standards and assessment, and policies are literally at the mercy of the teacher. At best they are means to an end. If they are to be useful, the teacher must like them, value their utility, and master the intricacies of their use. Thus, the wise leader recognizes that the teacher is the indispensable agent of curriculum reform.

Skillfully enhanced through a series of vignettes and case studies, the ideas set forth on the pages that follow are as much a treatise on leadership as curriculum activity, and rich in practical illustration. In distinguishing between education based on inner conviction and that based on outer conviction, the author's conviction is that coherent diversity, enlivened by the free spirit, can provide helpful alternatives to that which is scripted. In a time when formula and mandate threaten to dominate educational policy, the author's convictions provide a badly needed reminder that teaching should be a helping profession; that warmth, compassion, and common sense offer more virtue than blind obedience to one dogma or another; and that liberating vision stems from both the open eye and the open mind.

—Louis J. Rubin

Preface

Lee Shulman: At the heart of my work on good teaching is the notion of a teacher as an enlightened, passionate intellectual.

Carol Tell: Do you find that this notion goes against the trend these days to measure the success of students—and their teachers—by standardized test scores?

Lee Shulman: The confusion stems from valuing standards, on the one hand, and embodying those standards in high-stakes assessments, on the other.

The assessments end up corrupting the value of the standards. The standards get modified to be consistent with what we're able to measure in a high-stakes assessment. We have to ratchet down the standards and squeeze out all of the creative diversity because we want to be able to develop scoring keys that nobody can complain about or challenge.

—(Tell, 2001, pp. 6, 8)

John Dewey pointed out eons ago, there are two kinds of knowing: Knowledge we have gained on a conceptual level, and knowledge based on concrete experience, which becomes part of your psychological bloodstream.

—(Sarason, 2002, p. 60)

The newly elected superintendent of a large school system in the Southeast called his central-office staff together and briefly introduced them to his view of curriculum:

We need to identify those schools with low test scores after which we will do what needs to be done to bring about an incremental positive change in the scores. Because you are in charge of the curriculum and testing program, I will hold you accountable for raising the test scores. If you are successful, there will be plenty of money for you to attend conferences of your choice; if you are not, you will stay at home. Higher test scores will make us winners. I want to look like a winner.

The superintendent is a perfect example of what Lee Shulman, president of the Carnegie Foundation for the Advancement of Teaching and Professor at Stanford University, opposes in the header quote that introduced this preface. We can certainly not fault the superintendent for sending unclear signals to central office leaders. He made known a tangible outcome for schools—raise test scores. And he implicitly defined curriculum as a body of knowledge and skills to be ingested by students in order to raise test scores. We need to remind ourselves that test construction and distribution are a major component of curriculum construction and distribution. This is very big business. M. Scott Peck (1993, p. 232) uses the term *product vocation* to describe such ventures. Curriculum leadership, according to this superintendent, should focus on the technical creation of plans of study, which when taught effectively will raise test scores. His approach to curriculum is outside-in: An outside stimulus (curriculum as a course of study) is efficiently applied to an inside target (central office leaders, principals, teachers, and students) so that a desirable response (higher test scores) will make all concerned appear to be winners. The essentially political nature of the super-intendent's approach to these matters is revealed in his top-down, mandate-issuing governance style, a bureaucratic model for governance: (a) anticipate public reaction, (b) make the decision, and (c) implement the decision. Numbers, as revealed in higher test scores, make the superintendent appear to be a winner, and for their successful efforts central office leaders will be rewarded with resources to attend conferences. If central office leaders are not successful, they will be punished by having their travel funds cut.

The effect, intended or unintended, of the superintendent's approach to curriculum is to dehumanize the setting. Sociologist Max Weber describes this process:

> [Bureaucracy by] its special nature develops the more perfectly the more completely it succeeds in eliminating from official business love, hatred, and purely personal, irrational, and emotional elements which escape calculation. This is the specific nature of bureaucracy. (Gerth & Mills, 1946, pp. 215–216)

Gloria Steinem (1992, pp. 33–34) states this in a more personal way in her classic study of authority patterns, *Revolution From Within: A Book of Self-Esteem:* "Hierarchies try to convince us that all power and well-being come from the outside, that our self-esteem depends on obedience and measuring up to their requirements." Michael Fullan (2001), combining his expertise in school reform with organizational change and leadership, even in chaotic and uncontrollable situations, articulates *core values* required to lead. Being committed to such values and acting on the basis of them gives the leader the confidence and self-efficacy to creatively survive in educational bureaucracies—a challenge to the best of leaders.

What price do we pay for the dehumanization that exists in hierarchies? We deny ourselves the opportunity to directly encounter other persons. Instead of participating in the creative process, "we worship technique . . . as a way of evading the anxiety of the direct encounter" (May, 1975, p. 101). And those who define their roles primarily as political also pay a price. Hedrick Smith (1988, p. 92) describes this price: "Politicians strike me as a lonely crowd, making few deep friendships because almost every relationship is tainted by the calculus of power: How will this help me?" How sad this is given the fact that "The single factor common to every successful change initiative is that *relationships* improve" (Fullan, 2001, p. 5).

Let us now turn to an assistant principal in the South who has a different view of curriculum, one that entertains creativity in herself and others, and in the process involves her in the anxiety of the direct encounter. She demonstrates both the knowledge from conceptual experience and the knowledge based on concrete experience cited in the Sarason quote at the beginning of this preface.

Denise Hedrick, an assistant principal, is being interviewed for a middle school principalship. The first question she is asked is, "What are three key words that describe you?" She replies as follows:

> I have been recently undergoing a change in my value system, in large part because of my reading of Stephen Covey's *The 7 Habits of Highly Effective People.* This book has had a profound effect on me, and I am now in the process of evolving a new way of looking at myself, from the inside out. So to answer your question, the first key word that describes me is authentic. The second key word is integrity, which includes being honest, keeping promises, and fulfilling expectations. The third key word is proactive—taking the initiative to make things happen. What I really want to do as a leader is to create win–win situations. I know it takes time to do this but it pays off in the long run as opposed to rushing in and trying to fix things in a hurry.
>
> I have demonstrated as an assistant principal that I can make tough decisions in relating to various publics, but many difficult problems can be avoided through preventive actions. I can be very task oriented but the quality of the task performed depends on the quality of the person within.
>
> Sometimes I feel like Dorothy in *The Wizard of Oz.* I traveled so far only to find out that the answers were inside of me all along. My paradigm has shifted from focusing on the light that is directed at me, to focusing on the light that shines within me. Gloria Steinem helped me see that there is a difference between core self-esteem and situational self-esteem. As a result, I have a new clarity of purpose and a personal mission statement. Character is at the center of good leadership. (Hedrick, p. 3, 1993)

Denise brings passion to her work—an engagement with the excitement of learning and ideas. She has the blend of theory and practice, an engrossing pragmatism, described by Robert Fried in *The Passionate Teacher* (1996) and *The Passionate Learner* (2001). It is, as Fried says, an awakening of the person within. Denise also shares the pain and anguish that come with changing a value system (Kotter, 1996). A principal in reacting to Denise's journey said, "I discovered that I had to go past Good Friday to get to Easter."

The two approaches to leadership previously described force us to confront a major contradiction facing educational leaders in the United States today. External pressures are leveled at educators from many sides, but to simply structure one's life in response to such pressures is to risk feeling hollow within. The situational self-esteem afforded by higher test scores and other measures that make one *appear* to be a winner do little for the educator's core self-esteem. At the same time, however, the educational leader needs the political skills to deal realistically with external pressures.

In giving curriculum leadership seminars across the country, I have encountered a tremendous sense of sadness and a thirst for creativity and self-expression in relating to the contradiction described in the previous paragraph. Teachers and administrators want to nurture the sense of awe, wonder, and amazement that they experienced as curious children, turned on to the world around them (Sarason, 1993a). Yet they feel beaten down by external pressures that seek the quick fix. This same contradiction is evident in teacher and administrator preparation programs in colleges and universities (Sarason, 1993b, 2002).

The aim of *creative curriculum leadership* is to face this contradiction squarely and then shed light on ways in which today's educators can creatively lead others who confront the same dilemma. In the process of meeting this aim, a good deal of attention will be given to each person's *inner curriculum*, that is, one's sense of where he or she has been, is, and wants to be in the future. *Inner curriculum* is what one experiences as learning settings are cooperatively created. For too long this inner curriculum has been ignored, to the detriment of leaders and those led. One of the greatest gifts adult educators can give children, as well as others, is to build on the memory of what it was like to be a child. As Peck has stated so eloquently, "political power is a matter of externals and spiritual power a matter of what is within" (1993, p. 128). One must nurture *the inner curriculum* so that it serves as a foundation and reservoir for *outer curricula* (the course of study, largely symbolized by written materials such as textbooks, lesson plans, units of study, and the like), and one must create *outer curricula* that enhance the *inner curriculum*. Both must be viewed as organic and growing, and thus subject to change, rather than static and fixed. *The thesis or big idea presented in this book is that outer curriculum, the course of study, must be the best we can possibly select or create, but it is always a springboard to inner curriculum, what each person experiences as learning settings are cooperatively created.*

As creative curriculum leaders, we ask, "How can I understand myself better so that I enjoy my work and my life more?" and "How can I improve the settings or learning communities that are important to me?" Fortunately, there is no "right place" to begin our journey in answering these questions. The more I am meaningfully involved in activities within settings, the more I learn about myself—and vice versa. The only serious mistake is hiding from self and not giving leadership to the creation of learning settings.

A caveat needs to be added as we begin our study of creative curriculum leadership. We don't have the resources to be constantly analytical. Although we need to consider preventive steps, we also need to be aware of our culture and ourselves when things don't work out as they are supposed to, for it is precisely at this time that we need to know how our silent assumptions contribute to the problem (Schein, 1985). Sarason (2002) reminds us that *self-correction* is both a process and attitude, and the self-correcting process "is also a *problem-anticipating process*" (Sarason, p. 14).

In Part I, "The Meaning of Curriculum," Chapter 1 begins with a letter to the author from an educator in Charleston, South Carolina. The letter is provocative and poignant. She communicates the ways in which she has developed her own curriculum to integrate her professional and personal lives. In Chapter 2, "Defining Inner and Outer Curriculum," we search for a definition of curriculum that will help us reconcile the contradiction described at the beginning of this preface. The chapter leads us to the most common pitfall facing the educator involved in curriculum development—the view that development is a technical matter, with a set number of prescribed steps, rather than a creative artistic challenge. A related pitfall is the attitude that many involved in curriculum development have: "You should be where I am now." This attitude communicates the feeling that "I am above you and your problems and there is one right place to be in the curriculum development process." It belies the fact that development is a process in which each person unfolds gradually to grow and use a unique combination of talents and interests. The rescuer sometimes says, "You don't have to experience difficulties and pain like I did if you are where I'm at now." Yet it is precisely from experiencing pain and difficulties that we learn and grow through self-discipline (Peck, 1978). It is the special responsibility of our schools "to provide the tools and to develop the skills through which the child can create his or her own experience" (Eisner, 1988, p. 15).

Part II, "Education as Vocation: How a 'Sense of Calling' Influences Curriculum Development," places self within the context of vocation. Vocation does not mean job or career but rather refers to the original meaning of the Latin verb *vocare*, "to call." What is it that "called" you to creative curriculum leadership? What is it that sustains you to continue giving creative curriculum leadership? What is the role of developing your own curriculum in relation to your answers to the two previous questions? Chapter 3, "Learning From Your Professional Autobiography," challenges you, the reader, to view self as instrument in the curriculum leadership process (Combs, Avila, & Purkey, 1971). That is, creative curriculum leaders share with others (a) where they think they have been, (b) where they think they currently are, and (c) where they would like to be in the future. A number of self-appraisal inventories are used to face this challenge.

The interesting thing about being engaged in "know thyself" leadership activities is that you will hear and therefore discover more about yourself in front of others. This process of defining ourselves empowers us rather than letting others do this for us (Steinem, 1992). Empowerment of self is essential before significant changes or transformation can occur.

One of the main ways in which we empower ourselves and others is to enjoy the core of our work so much that we communicate this to others in our verbal and nonverbal actions. Chapter 4, "Looking Forward to Work: The Power of Wanting to Be There," treats this important matter by sharing, in a student's own words, how she knows whether her teachers want to be with her. "Keeping the Fire in Your Vocation," Chapter 5, suggests ways in which we can avoid or work our way out of burnout.

Part III, "Curriculum Development Can Make a Difference," presents concrete ways in which each of us can relate to self, others, and the environment as we develop curriculum. Chapter 6, "Creative Curriculum Leadership in Practice," defines such leadership as using our talents to help others identify and use their talents. Most definitions of leadership have a highly manipulative ring to them: "The secret is to get others to do what you want them to do whether they want to do it or not." Such definitions don't give members of a setting the feeling that they own the directions in which they are going. "Civility in Leadership: The Ultimate Difference," Chapter 7, presents the view that creative leaders set the stage by giving attention to civilities within the setting. Such civilities are an essential norm in the creation of curriculum within community (Peck, 1993). Civilities are much more than manners and politeness; they must reflect the creative curriculum leader's basic character traits, such as honesty and integrity.

Chapter 8, "Creating Learning Communities," challenges the creative curriculum leader to help others build their *social capital* as they follow their interests and talents. The changing nature of culture and society with regard to participation in communities provides the context for the leadership efforts of educators interested in creating learning communities. You will see throughout this book that the creation of settings and learning communities is a major theme and thesis. In fact, "community building is the ideal vehicle for the teaching of civility" (Peck, 1993, p. 284). It is in building community that we practice civility. The creative curriculum leader's motto could well be "community building first, decision making second" (Peck, 1993, p. 286). Chapter 9, "Teacher Leaders," guides the reader in rethinking teachers' work. A promising feature of the educational landscape is the opportunity for teachers to participate actively in the shaping of school and school-system culture. Teacher leadership is valuable in its own right, and it has the added value that many of today's teacher leaders will be tomorrow's assistant principals, principals, and superintendents.

Readers will find cases (critical incidents) designed to stimulate thinking and discussion at the end of the chapters. The cases pick up on the problems and dilemmas in each chapter. In field testing these cases with hundreds of teachers and administrators in leadership seminars, we have discovered that these members of the school community want to be actively involved in applying ideas from each chapter to settings in which they are leaders; cases are an excellent way to bridge theory and practice. They are the next best thing to being there. You are invited to identify possible responses from which you choose a preferred response and rationale for it. Then compare and contrast your response and rationale to the author's preferred response and rationale. We have found in using these cases that they can stimulate educators to make informed decisions that can have a lasting effect on self and others. The reader will also note that there are curriculum leadership and learning activities in this book's appendices. The reader may simply react to the activities while reading this book or may use the materials in leading professional development seminars.

We have been happily surprised to discover a larger and more diverse audience for this book than we expected. Book reviews, e-mails, letters, and phone calls from a variety of creative curriculum leaders have been most heartening: superintendents, central office leaders, principals, assistant principals, teachers, special education leaders, gifted education leaders, religious education leaders, nursing educators, and others in higher education. The responses from readers who conduct leadership seminars in general and curriculum leadership seminars in particular have also been gratifying and helpful in the revision of the book. Seminar leaders have found many creative ways to share the basic concepts from this book with seminar participants. Their basic message is that we need to create communities of learners who will give attention to each person's inner curriculum.

Many educators were important in writing this book. Special appreciation is due to the leaders who field tested the cases in seminars. *Intercultural Interactions*, by Richard W. Brislin, Kenneth Cushner, Craig Cherrie, and Mehealana Yong, was the model for the format used in identifying responses to cases. Any author knows the value of an excellent editor. Fortunately, I have such an editor in Kylee Liegl, whose northern Michigan roots I share. Finally, Douglas Rife, president and publisher of Corwin Press, has carried on the fine pioneering efforts of Gracia A. Alkema by building a staff that knows the game and the score. Douglas, like Gracia, has resisted the lure of hierarchical relationship in favor of collegial "thinking out loud" conversations, and as a result, the author discovers new and exciting ways to share ideas and feelings with the reader. In short, they live creative leadership as it is described in this book—a gift to all of us.

Finally, I wish to issue an invitation to the reader. If you wish to extend our conversation about ideas in this book, please e-mail me at dlbrubak@uncg.edu

I promise a response.

About the Author

Dale L. Brubaker is a professor of education at the University of North Carolina at Greensboro. He previously served on the faculties of the University of Wisconsin, Milwaukee and the University of California, Santa Barbara. He is the author or coauthor of numerous books including *Creative Survival in Educational Bureaucracies, Curriculum Planning: The Dynamics of Theory and Practice, Teacher as Decision-Maker* (Corwin), *Staying on Track* (Corwin), *Theses and Dissertations,* and *Avoiding Thesis and Dissertation Pitfalls.* He received his B.A. from Albion College and his M.A. and Ph.D. from Michigan State University

**CORWIN
PRESS**

The Corwin Press logo—a raven striding across an open book—represents the union of courage and learning. Corwin Press is committed to improving education for all learners by publishing books and other professional development resources for those serving the field of K–12 education. By providing practical, hands-on materials, Corwin Press continues to carry out the promise of its motto: "**Helping Educators Do Their Work Better.**"

Prologue

A Cautionary Tale

Ken was a bright young man whose exemplary elementary school teaching and leadership made him stand out from the crowd. He quickly became the lead teacher in his school. Guided by his principal, he pursued and received a master's degree in school administration. First hired as an assistant principal in the elementary school where he did his internship, a year later he assumed the principalship. He continued his higher education studies as a doctoral student at the same time he began his first year as an elementary school principal, in a program that led him to research and writing on the major issues facing today's elementary school principal.

When the summer institute for newly appointed school principals took place, Ken and others were given the following advice: *PROCEED WITH CAUTION THE FIRST YEAR. THIS IS THE TIME TO LISTEN AND LEARN!* Ken took this advice and absorbed all that he could about key issues facing the elementary school principal, especially with regard to curriculum and instruction. The first thing Ken was alerted to was the strong external pressure on the principal and elementary schools in particular—even stronger than when he was a teacher leader. The accountability movement, state standards, and assessment were a reality to be ignored at the principal's peril. Not only did his state have mandated gateway standards at the third, fifth, and eighth grades, but there was new federal pressure as well. The No Child Left Behind (NCLB)

Act of 2001 required states to test all students in reading and math each year in grades 3 through 8 and at least once in high school. This act was a marker event in that it mandated school-level accountability for all students' learning. Because this learning took place in classrooms, individual educators and students were held accountable.

Ken was aware that the year before he had assumed the principalship, his school district was in trouble with regard to NCLB federal standards. Several subgroups had fallen short of standards in grades 4 and 8. Only 59 percent of children who qualified for free or reduced-price lunches passed fourth-grade reading, with math scores also well behind other students. Limited-English students missed nearly all of the benchmarks, and African American students didn't meet the benchmarks in fourth-grade reading and eighth-grade math, lagging more than 20 percent behind white students in both areas.

The achievement gap between the district's Hispanic and white students also widened. The district was warned to make progress in closing the gap or it would face sanctions. If a single subgroup within a school fell below the minimum passing rates established by the state, the entire school would fail to meet its NCLB goals. Schools that missed even one of the federal standards for one or more consecutive years would suffer sanctions, including letting students transfer to a school of their choice. A special challenge faced the district in that less than half of disabled fourth graders passed the state reading test. Many of the students with learning disabilities were not exempted from the NCLB requirements.

These events provided Ken with a challenge.

Advocates of new accountability measures argued that the following benefits would emerge. The achievement gap between the "haves" and the "have-nots"—primarily children of color and low-income homes—would be narrowed. Expectations for the "have-nots" would be high but realizable, thus stimulating teachers to do their best to reach such children. Traditional generalizations about students from good homes being successful and children from low-income homes being unsuccessful would be challenged rather than simply accepted. Teaching communities would be constructed to reach these important goals with collaborative teaching and learning serving as an important vehicle for raising student achievement. Scores would go up as students and faculty discovered they could overcome what were previously felt to be obstacles.

As might be expected, however, research findings on such matters were mixed. Ken saw that the uniqueness of each educational setting made it difficult to prescribe remedies across the board with a one-size-fits-all approach.

Critics of the new mandates argued that high-stakes testing brought out the worst in competitive educators, some of whom turned to one or more "testing irregularities"—a euphemism for cheating. In these cases, a school's overall scores would be raised by excluding certain children. A central-office testing coordinator and a few teachers in Ken's system were forced into retirement; an assistant principal was fired because of such alleged behavior.

Other problems arose in trying to align district standards with state standards. The state had set broad learning goals and had constructed tests to judge how well students were meeting them. The district then created a curriculum and a series of classroom tests to be sure that students were moving toward the achievement of state goals. Critics of such alignment procedures argued that the curriculum was shrunk to fit itself. In other words, only what was measured got done. Teachers taught to the test, thus limiting learning to only those items relevant to it. District tests were formatted to match state tests. Playing the testing game was especially pronounced on the part of beginning teachers, who were anxious about surviving in a highly competitive environment. Many creative teachers, it can be argued, left teaching because of externally imposed standardization of curriculum and instruction. Their professional judgment was replaced by politicians' mandates as translated by testing people at the state department of education.

Ken knew that he couldn't ignore either side of the debate. He was a caring professional who knew the upside and downside of competition and the importance of being a professional person. Yet he was reminded that each person's dignity and developmental readiness must be respected.

What, then, were Ken's options with regard to these matters? Ken had struggled mightily and listened to many colleagues' views in answering this question. Although some principals Ken talked to supported detailed intervention strategies designed to raise test scores, it was difficult to convey the pain many principals experienced in working through these issues. As one seasoned principal told Ken, "My job is to keep external pressures from entering the door of our school. There is simply too much junk out there, with its advocates trying to get into our school. My job is to help teachers teach well. The test scores will take care of themselves." This philosophy seemed to work at this school, where 95 percent of students received free or reduced-price lunches, because test scores had steadily risen in the five years the principal had been there. A fellow doctoral student and elementary school principal argued in a similar vein: "A telltale sign of a principal in trouble was when I visited his or her school and was told 'We have terrible test scores here.' I responded, 'Show me,' and nine times out of ten they couldn't find the scores. They had what I would call 'amorphous anxiety.' "

Ken was clear on one matter: He was the gatekeeper for his school. He believed that it was his responsibility to simplify communications from the central office, the state department of public instruction, and elsewhere. He also knew it was unwise to give people packages of information all at once. He knew what was going on in the school as a whole, and in classrooms in particular, because he spent most of his time visiting classes rather than working in his office.

Ken firmly believed that his core values and beliefs were the foundation for everything he did as a principal and person. Michael Fullan's *Leading in a Culture of Change* (2001), with its emphasis on moral purpose and core values, was important to Ken as he has assessed his own leadership as a teacher-leader and assistant principal. He had worked with his faculty members individually and in large and small groups so that school goals were as consistent with his core values as they could be. He frequently talked to teachers and others about how the assessment of students, teachers, and staff must be consistent with the goals of the school. Without this, he reminded others, his "house," a schoolhouse, was built on sand. What, then, were Ken's core values or beliefs?

First of all, Ken knew that each student, as well as each member of the faculty and staff, contributed to the school and each other in ways that cannot always be measured or at times even known. Numbers only tell part of the story. This perspective on Ken's part prompted him to find ways to honor publicly faculty, staff members, students, and parents for their contributions. He constantly reminded himself to catch people doing things right rather than falling into the critic's role of focusing on what was missing or wrong—the deficit model.

Second, Ken understood and valued the diverse nature of the contributions of adults and children. The talents they brought to school—talents that they sometimes didn't even recognize in themselves—frequently surprised him. And, once again, he publicly honored the diverse and unique talents they demonstrated. Ken learned the difference between common definitions of leadership that refer to getting people to do what you wanted them to do, whether or not they wanted to do it, and creative leadership in which the leader uses his or her talents to help others recognize and use their talents.

Third, Ken knew that the creation of learning settings was the key to true community and that everyone interested in his school should be invited to be included in such communities. Ken wanted to make special efforts to involve parents and other community members in the life of the school. He knew that when he was a fellow learner, others found such cooperative learning contagious. His ego was in check as he focused on matters outside of himself. It was a joyful and reciprocal process. Ken believed that "Lone Rangers" would not be comfortable in his school. At the same time, he knew that educators needed time to themselves. To be apart from community at times was not the same as being a distant person.

Fourth, Ken wanted to involve faculty and staff in conversations about what, from all of the programs and materials aimed at his school, would be enduring as opposed to those that would simply be "flavor of the month" fads. In his own mind, multiple intelligences and moral education were at the top of his list of priorities because without them, basic skills have a shaky foundation. Ken was wary of new superintendents who came into a school system like "gangbusters" with a new curriculum fad to be forced on all who worked there. He knew that such superintendents would be held accountable for programs introduced but probably wouldn't be around for the programs' evaluations. At the same time, he had the common political sense to know when to speak up and when to be quiet about such behavior. He picked the places and times to stand up for what he felt could be accomplished.

Fifth, Ken recognized and valued creating the best formal curriculum possible, the course of study that served as a springboard to real learning that took place *within* persons—their inner curriculums. He believed that the best teachers plant seeds that they may never see bloom; digging up the seeds every couple of hours to see if they are growing kills them. It was this belief that made Ken place the hiring and supporting of dedicated and seasoned educators high on his agenda.

How did Ken relate to externally imposed curriculum and instruction mandates? He recognized the reality of their existence, but he weighed all of his decisions in relation to his core beliefs and values stated in the preceding paragraphs. He understood *what is* and *what should be,* and he continued to struggle mightily to bring about *what can be*—always within the context in which he gave leadership. Ken was aware that he had to be able to identify and articulate practical alternatives to his teachers and others. In addition, Ken was especially conscious of the challenge he and his teachers would face in identifying and analyzing assumptions underlying proposals with regard to student achievement. This was why Ken and the teachers in the school had to be able to identify and analyze their own basic assumptions as they went about their work in curriculum and instruction. Ken used the iceberg metaphor to demonstrate the power of underlying assumptions: "Seven-eighths of the iceberg is below the waterline, with only one-eighth visible to the observer. We must move below the tip of the iceberg to get at the tacit or understood assumptions." The example he gave brought this idea home: "Few teachers tell us that we have sent them the wrong children but their behavior, the tip of the iceberg, demonstrates that they feel this way! We must get them to be conscious of the basic assumptions that they bring to the instructional setting for them to have a chance to change their attitudes and behavior."

Ken never forgot the lessons he learned when he was "in the trenches" as an elementary schoolteacher. He knew first-hand the pain and suffering that often resulted from wrestling with the contradictions one faced as a teacher. Because he learned from his experiences and shared a common language with teachers as well as the experiences they faced on a daily basis, he had a great deal of credibility with his staff members.

As a doctoral student, one of Ken's professors took him backstage into the world of assessment. Sam Miller helped Ken see that the state mandates testing, but it does not mandate the purchasing of test-preparation materials, nor does it mandate the testing of students every nine weeks as some principals do. Miller suggested an alternative perspective would be to teach students so that they would do well on any test. Two schools in the district, with different student populations, adopted this philosophy with successful results. Ken and Professor Miller believed that when the amount of time spent practicing for tests became a curriculum in itself, students were missing out on a quality education. Ken's knowledge of the testing process and his plan for relating to high-stakes testing enhanced his already high credibility.

Engaged in the "nitty-gritty" of student assessment, Ken met with teachers individually and in small groups, largely by grade level, to analyze data. He sought teachers' ideas as to how to improve curriculum and instruction. Together, they discussed how children could learn test-taking skills—for example, answer items that you know first and then turn to other items that need attention. Ken made every effort to have testing people in central office come into the school to explain tests, test scores, and what those scores meant. He went out of his way to attend regional and state seminars on student assessment. He also turned to a few principals who were more knowledgeable than he was on the details of student assessment in general and testing in particular to get answers to his questions. Ken was convinced, after reading Michael Fullan (2001), that interpersonal relationships as well as knowledge creation and sharing were central to the learning settings he gave leadership to as the principal of his school.

Unlike some principals, Ken had overall perspective on accountability measures as well as curriculum and instruction. Three questions served him well in his struggle to make sense out of what was going on in today's elementary schools: *What is worth knowing? Who presently decides what is worth knowing?* And, *who should decide what is worth knowing?* Ken's courses and other experiences as a doctoral student were helpful as he sought answers.

Ken's own professionalism served as an example that spoke volumes to those he led. He pointed out to his teachers on many an occasion that the teacher as a professional must have long-term commitments to worthy goals; there were no quick fixes that could keep a professional from doing work over the long haul. It would take courage to do this. Faculty members noted and respected Ken's willingness to work as hard or harder than they over a sustained period of time. They understood he wouldn't be their principal for a year or two to simply build up his resume. Finally, Ken's intelligence, love of ideas, and ability to articulate them gave the elementary school a sense of presence that made a difference in the community and in the school system's central office. When teachers needed an answer or advocate for their ideas, Ken would step forward and represent them in an effective way. He could be counted on for answers, and teachers were secure in knowing that the formal head of the school would represent them well in public forums.

Ken and others in his school received a bonus for their efforts when the director of testing informed Ken that the school's test scores increased from the previous year, with teachers and assistants receiving a small financial reward for their efforts. Although Ken and his lead teachers knew that test scores were not the only indicator of learning, they recognized the political and morale value of improved test scores as an indication of current improvement and continuing progress.

PART I

The Meaning of Curriculum

Activity in itself is not satisfying for any period of time. Meaning must be associated with our activity. For example, if you are given the assignment of moving sandbags from Place A to Place B and then from Place B to Place A simply to keep you busy, you will soon become bored with the task. If, on the other hand, you move sandbags from Place A to Place B (your front yard) to keep back floodwaters, you will indeed find meaning in the activity.

So it is with developing curriculum as *a course of study*. This construction work must be meaningful to you, the builder, and the product you produce (the course of study) must also be a springboard that will stimulate personal meaning for those who use it.

The two major questions facing the creative curriculum leader, questions that link the inner curriculum (*what each person experiences as learning settings are cooperatively created*) and the outer curriculum (*the course of study*), are the following: How shall I live with myself? and, How shall we live with each other? (Brubaker, 1989; Macdonald, 1977).

Chapter 1, "Introduction: Developing One's Own Curriculum," begins with an account of an educator's struggle to reconcile the inner and outer curricula. It is a creative curriculum leader's effort to locate authority in herself as well as in external forces.

Chapter 2, "Defining Inner and Outer Curriculum," discusses two definitions of curriculum, inner and outer, and the implications of these definitions for the creative curriculum leader. The chapter argues that both definitions have their place and that we are challenged to create new and useful relationships between them.

The main goal of the two chapters is to update you, the reader, on the exciting activity of creative curriculum leadership.

1

Introduction

Developing One's Own Curriculum

When we say that someone is a student, whether in the first grade or in high school, we tend to be more impressed with what they do not know and cannot do than with what they do know and are interested in.

—Seymour B. Sarason (1993a, p. 190)

The title of this book, *Creative Curriculum Leadership*, as well as the immediate inspiration for writing it, came from a letter from Teri Gainey Bastian, an educator in Charleston, South Carolina. The letter, a sensitive and at times poignant account of her efforts to develop her own curriculum, bears quoting in its entirety, after which we will explore its meaning.

I want to share with you my observations for the past few years in the area of curriculum development. I decided to write you on the ride home with friends after your lecture on creative curriculum leadership so that I wouldn't forget anything. These ideas come from three primary areas: my career, my cousin, and my hobby.

Many of my colleagues and I bemoan the fact that the things we learned in our courses taken for the master's degree in education touch only a very small part of what we actually do on the job. What has been most helpful to us has been attending conventions, talking to each other, attending workshops, and reading literature. In order to be really effective on our jobs we have needed far more information, experience, and stimulation than we had in our master's degree program.

At first I resented this fact. Then I realized that my cousin, who is a highly respected and nationally recognized CPA, has done something very similar within his vocation. He attends local, state, and national conventions. He reads leadership, management, and accounting literature constantly (even when he's grilling steaks). He participates on a national scale in peer review programs. *In short, he continuously is developing his own curriculum.*

As a hobby, I am an artist. Because I never drew anything but stick people until about eighteen years ago, I decided to develop my own curriculum rather than entering a bachelor's degree program. I am an active member of three artist guilds. I attend workshops in areas of art that interest me. My entertainment budget goes to art books and magazine subscriptions. I also experiment with and fail at loads of art projects. I love not getting a grade from a teacher. Some people are very drawn to my work, but others are not. Mostly, though, I like it. I never took the first art course when I was in college because I was so fearful of not being good at it. I know that a traditional art curriculum with a teacher judging my work would have ended my talent development. Instead, I love my art and actually sell quite a bit of it.

In being part of an innovative doctoral program, I have found a university that truly makes learning relevant to my work and life as a whole. I am constantly reminded of a poster of a giraffe that I had in my classroom with the inscription "Learning Is Life Long." I know that my life, no matter how long it lasts, will never be long enough to see and learn and do all the things I want.

Thanks for the invitation to write to you. This opportunity was a grand way to cope with the problem of the long ride home.

Sincerely,
Teri Gainey Bastian

P.S. I loved laughing and singing with you and my colleagues today. It was a once in a lifetime opportunity, but I wish it happened more. That's something I can do [something] about, isn't it?

THE LETTER'S MEANING

Teri Gainey Bastian's words have the ring of truth because she writes from her experience in relating to universities and schools. In fact, the first thing we note is that curriculum as a course of study is an important but relatively minor part of her curriculum development. Another way to say this is that she places her own learning first. She sees herself at the center of learning rather than simply locating authority in external sources, such as textbooks and professors' lecture notes. She views her role as an actor who is motivated internally, rather than a reactor who is motivated externally. *As Gloria Steinem says, self-authority is the single most radical idea there is, and there is a real hunger for putting the personal and the external back together again* (Attinger, 1992, p. 55). The revolutionary nature of this thought is clear when one realizes that placing her own learning first runs counter to both the role of the student in university culture and the culture of the schools.

The higher the level of schooling, the more the student is taught to devalue his or her own insights and to value the insights of those whose ideas are considered to be more worthy. This may be in part because secondary schools are so much larger and more bureaucratized than earlier grades (Sarason, 1971). Likewise, high school teachers tend to emulate their best university professors, who are seen as purveyors of knowledge to be ingested by students. For example, imagine a doctoral student who has selected a topic for a research paper or dissertation and begins the project by writing down all he or she knows on the subject. The very idea seems ludicrous, for we have all been advised to begin doing research by going to the library or doing a literature search on the views of others.

The K–8 educator is pressured in another direction. School buses and central-office public relations officials advertise as follows: *Children First* and *Schools Are for Children.* In short, high school and university classrooms place the student in the role of an empty vessel to be filled with ideas from external authorities, while K–8 classrooms tend to define the teacher as a missionary ministering to the lives of children. The effect of both cultures is to give the educator a secondary learning role. At the same time, it is both common sense and part of education folklore that a teacher or administrator turned on to learning will probably create a climate in which others are more likely to be turned on to learning. This is simply one of the contradictions in education that can be detrimental to educators and students alike.

It is also true that problem solving, one of the major pedagogical approaches in schools and universities, is based on a deficit model: We focus on what is missing or wrong to the exclusion of what is right and should be preserved. One of the reasons for this is that problem-solving approaches begin with the question "What is the problem?" rather than "How do *I* experience the problem?" The administrator or teacher, for example, usually senses the pain associated with a serious problem before framing the question "What is the problem?" Educators often feel one or more of the following maladies when facing a serious problem: stomachaches, overeating, being unable to eat, headaches, inability to concentrate, and waking up in a cold sweat. Yet they are not asked to begin the problem-solving process by sharing such personally important experiences; rather, they are asked to move immediately to higher-level thinking processes by focusing on questions such as, "What is the problem?" and "What alternative solutions are open to you?" The removal of the student's experiences from Teri Gainey Bastian's master's program courses is one of the reasons the courses touch only a small part of what we (master's students) do on the job (as educators).

Ralph Waldo Emerson stated the case for the primacy of experience in his "Essay on History," written in 1903:

> We are always coming up with the emphatic facts of history in our private experience and verifying them here. All history becomes subjective; in other words there is properly no history, only biography. Every mind must know the whole lesson for itself—must go over the whole ground. What it does not see, what it does not live, it will not know. (p. 10)

Eliot Eisner confirms Emerson's thesis by stating, "It is the qualities we experience that provide the content through which meaning is secured" (Eisner, 1988, p. 16). Likewise, Emerson's and Eisner's arguments for the primacy of experience is supported by Rollo May: "Thinking and self-creating are inseparable" (May, 1975, p. 116).

Because of an inadequate master's degree program, Teri, like her CPA cousin, adopted a proactive stance and developed her own curriculum, consisting of attending conventions, talking to others in her field, attending workshops, and reading literature. Furthermore, she continued to develop her own curriculum by using similar vehicles to become an artist, a hobby that stimulates her entire professional and personal life.

It is in doing art that Teri most dramatically follows her bliss. As a member of three artist guilds, she is part of support communities. She avoids the judgmentalism of grading by not taking courses in which grades are assigned. In her own words, "I know a traditional art curriculum with a teacher 'judging' my work would have ended my talent development." Rather, she attends workshops that interest her and uses her entertainment budget to buy art books and magazine subscriptions. She recognizes that artistic expression leads to mixed reviews from critics. She has reconciled this contradiction by concluding, "I love my art." In short, she has located authority in herself rather than in the judgments of others.

In locating authority in herself and her experiences, Teri yearns for and has achieved in large measure an integration of her learning. Such integration is challenged by a segmented view of curriculum in courses in high schools and universities.

The position that each course's learning must be discrete was brought home to me during the final semester of my undergraduate education. During that year, I experienced one of those rare moments when the learning from a variety of courses came together in a comprehensible and meaningful whole. European history, world drama, world literature, art appreciation, and world religions made sense to me in ways that were simply amazing. I sat down and wrote what I considered to be one of the best essay examination answers within my experience. The next day, the professor of the world religions class called and asked me to stop by his office for a conference. "I simply can't grade your exam," he said. Then he added, "I only wanted you to write what you had learned in this class." I left his office with a C + for the most meaningful examination I had ever written." There is often a price for locating authority in self. One upsets the normal order of things, which can be painful to self and others. A letter from a college student to his mother illustrates this point:

Dear Mom,

I'm really enjoying college. Last week I learned how to ski for the first time and broke a leg. Thank heavens it wasn't mine.

Love,
Mike

It is important to make a distinction between the need for curriculum as a course of study and our evaluation of a particular course of study. Teri does not criticize the need for curriculum as a course of study, but she is wary of a traditional approach to curriculum because, in her view, it only locates authority outside the learner. Form, something that sets limits by excluding parts of objective reality, provides the essential boundaries and structure for the creative act (May, 1975, p. 140). George S. Counts, noted educator and colleague of John Dewey, said this in a humorous way: "The reason I want my children raised as Methodists is so that they have something to reject" (Brubaker, 1989, p. 109). In other words, form and boundaries of the Methodist faith would give his children something to react to so that they could build their own faith. Limiting and expanding thus go together (May, 1975, p. 137). Discipline and creative imagination struggle in a kind of dialectic that must be reconciled by the creative curriculum leader—without the conflict and struggle, there would be no exercise of human intelligence.

CONCLUSION

One of the reasons Teri Gainey Bastian's letter is so powerful is that her ideas and feelings about curriculum development rest on a vision for learning that nurtures the curiosity all humans have from our earliest days (Sarason, 1993b). By assuming the leadership for her own learning, she develops her own curriculum. This doesn't discount curriculum as a course of study in schools and universities. It does, however, challenge us to define curriculum as a course of study in such a way that it is a springboard that releases our natural curiosity and our desire to own what is created. The next chapter speaks to the importance of defining curriculum.

Case 1: Choosing a Graduate School

After several years of experience as an educator, you feel ready to pursue graduate study. Your choice of graduate schools is between a traditional one and an innovative satellite program. Both are within an hour's driving distance and are credentialed by the state, so your economic benefits from completion of the degree are assured. You decide to attend recruitment and orientation sessions in the spring before your enrollment.

The speaker at the more traditional university summarizes the benefits as follows: (a) The program of study is established so that those who hire and promote you in your school system will be familiar with everything you do during graduate study; (b) there is a well-established library with excellent computer services; (c) professors don't come and go and can be counted on to see you through your program; (d) the curriculum (course of study) changes little from year to year, thus affording you security; and (e) administrators and professors have established networks to help you get jobs throughout the state.

The speaker for the satellite program is equally articulate and also summarizes the advantages of the innovative university: (a) You will be one of a group of pioneers whose enthusiasm and sense of community will be contagious; (b) computers will give you access to the information you need as a scholar on your feet so that you don't need a traditional library; (c) professors aren't tenured, and you will get fresh ideas rather than hearing the same old ideas from the same professors; (d) your experiences in the work world will be part of the innovative curriculum; and (e) graduates from other satellite programs within the university will afford you access to a national network for employment opportunities.

Which university program will you enroll in for fall classes? Please choose the best response from the alternatives that follow:

1. I will enroll in the traditional graduate program.

2. I will enroll in the satellite graduate program.

3. I will spend another semester or year investigating this matter.

Case 1: Rationales for the Alternative Responses

1. It is simply too risky to enroll in a nontraditional graduate program. Remember, pioneers are the ones who get arrows in their backs. You will benefit from the security and prestige of the traditional university, even though the economic benefits from the two university programs are identical. Graduates from the traditional university will support you when you graduate. After all, they have a vested interest in their own degree from the traditional university. Professors at the traditional university are a known quantity, and you can use your network of graduates to learn how to negotiate the degree program in an efficient way. If you opt for security over all else, the traditional university program is a good choice, but the tremendous changes in our society should prompt you to consider other choices.

2. It is hypocritical to talk about changes in our society and world as an educator while at the same time enrolling in a traditional program for reasons of security and prestige. The innovative program will give you an opportunity to build a bridge between your work world and the university. Because professors aren't tenured, the satellite university won't have to keep deadwood: You have to wake up some tenured professors to pay them. Because economic benefits and credentials are identical from the two universities, this is not a matter of concern. With regard to prestige, once you buy into pecking-order thinking, there is no end to believing that this is better than that. Instead of focusing on what needs to be done, you give resources to trying to get and keep others' approval. Other graduates from satellite programs will have the enthusiasm of pioneers and will therefore actively help you find employment opportunities. To attend the innovative university program is a good choice.

3. Waiting a semester or year will give you a chance to gather more information. You will then have a stronger feeling about the rightness of your choice. The difficulty with this decision is that those who tend to put off a decision lose the benefits of taking the initiative. Being proactive and then keeping the momentum are the keys to successful completion of a graduate program. Get on with it. Consider a better choice.

2

Defining Inner and Outer Curriculum

Curriculum is the environment in the school and in the classroom. You have there in miniature what you have in life outside of the classroom and the school. Curriculum is therefore life! That's why it is so vital and exciting. That's what makes it important. There's nothing out there that doesn't relate to curriculum.

—James B. Macdonald (1977)

We do not operate directly in reality but instead act on the basis of our maps (theories) of reality. According to Jürgen Habermas (1971), our major human interests are located in one of three places: control, understanding, or liberation. The primary orientation of each person's conception of curriculum planning, an essential part of creative curriculum leadership, is in one of these three places.

CONCEPTIONS OF CURRICULUM PLANNING

If you are an educator, your first methods of teaching class imprinted in your mind the proper map for instruction and learning as well as the appropriate definition of curriculum. In fact, every teaching methods textbook used in teacher preparation classes has been organized according to this map or theory of pedagogical reality.

Think for a moment of the first lesson plan you ever wrote. You were taught to organize this lesson plan as follows: (a) select and behavioralize objectives, (b) select and organize activities (methods and materials) for student learning, and (c) evaluate the effectiveness of activities in reaching objectives (Tyler, 1949). This is referred to as the *Tyler rationale*. You were taught that there is a proper sequence to be followed to be a successful teacher. At a deeper level, you were assured you would not fail if you tried at all times to control the classroom environment in general and students in particular. If this sounds like a masculine, take-charge, rational approach, you have interpreted it correctly (Lightfoot, 1983). Gloria Steinem (1992) speaks to this gender-related matter:

> I had been raised to assume all power was outside myself, but they [men] had been raised to place power almost nowhere but within themselves. Often, they were suffering too. Just as the fantasy of no control was the enemy of my self-esteem, the fantasy of total control was the enemy of theirs. (p. 22)

The technology of teaching rests on a scientific conception of pedagogy, the symbol of which is the number. Counting outcomes and producing rates is synonymous with being rational (Bogdan & Biklen, 1982, p. 116).

Curriculum leaders who are primarily interested in control speak in terms of an efficient educational system. A technically sound system, it is argued, will demonstrate progress in measurable terms. I am amazed and disquieted by the number of superintendents who use the terms *evaluation* and *measurement* synonymously, whereas, in fact, measurement is but one kind of evaluation or assessment. If our discussion of the control mode sounds like industrial or factory rhetoric, it is because this language originated in the early years of the Industrial Revolution. Alvin Toffler (1980), in his classic work, *The Third Wave*, describes how Second Wave civilization, or industrial civilization, relies on measurement to prove that progress is inevitable (pp. 114–131). Thus, our allegiance to measurement is based on several myths that hold an industrial society together. To challenge such myths is to challenge those wedded to an industrial view of civilization.

The formula-driven Tyler rationale is obviously linear and sequential. This provides comfort, security, and the feeling of control. The curriculum planner knows what to do and in what order to do it. Any curriculum planning challenge is a problem that can be solved with the proper organizational tools. The idea that some problems are dilemmas to be reconciled is foreign to the curriculum planner as controller. The efficiency expert must provide leadership in task-oriented settings. Followers in turn share the leader's (manager's) unquestioned faith that the setting can and should be controlled at all times. This implies that persons within such settings must be controlled and monitored in the interest of efficiency.

A curriculum leader, interested in implementing the control theory during the Management by Objectives (MBO) era, describes her enthusiasm for the movement:

> I was inwardly proud that I was asked to attend the conference, but I was anxious about the fact that my superintendent of schools would also attend. It was a 2-day conference on management by objectives. The curriculum conference leader introduced MBO by pointing out that Henri Fayol, a French industrialist, identified what he called management essentials in the year 1916. These essentials were planning, organization, command, coordination, and control. The conference leader informed the group that his experience with MBO proved its usefulness in any setting. He listed seven questions that the effective MBO leader should ask:
>
> 1. What needs to be done?
> 2. What are the best ways to do these things?
> 3. When must these things be done?

4. What resources will be needed?

5. What will constitute satisfactory performance?

6. How much progress will this lead to?

7. What changes will be needed to improve performance?

I was impressed with the simplicity and practicability of the MBO design. This design is one that will be supported by my staff for it will give them something to get their teeth into and they will see their progress. I also like the optimism in the plan. We can't go wrong.

While at the conference I had time to revise many of the charts distributed by the conference leader. I will use these charts to plot the progress of curriculum-leadership groups throughout the year.

Now that you have been introduced to the control orientation toward curriculum and curriculum planning, let us summarize criticisms of this approach:

1. Control is but one human interest, and it is appropriate for nonhuman rather than human subjects (Macdonald, 1980, p. 2).

2. As with all technical approaches, attention is given to linear, sequential processes but not to basic assumptions below such processes.

3. This orientation fits the industrial view, and this simply reinforces the status quo. It doesn't speak to the tremendous changes that have taken place in a postindustrial Information Age society. Information, for example, bombards people in simultaneous rather than linear, sequential ways.

Disenchantment with the limited scientific and technical dimensions of control theory has prompted some curriculum-planning leaders and scholars to give more attention to the humanities. Conceptual frameworks have been developed to stimulate interpretations and perspectives as alternatives to the 1949 Tyler rationale.

The methodology of hermeneutics (understanding) has led many scholars to reject much of the scientific-technical language of control theorists in favor of less restrictive ways of conversing about curriculum and curriculum planning (Brubaker, 1989; Macdonald, 1980). One of the reasons for these conversations is that our experience tells us we usually learn more as educators when things are somewhat out of control. That is, we are challenged by surprises despite the fact that we try to avoid such surprises. Patrick Welsh (1987), author of *Tales out of School*, describes this matter: "The books on pedagogy stress the importance of control in the classroom. But it's often when things are a little out of control when I get a queasy feeling in my stomach that real learning takes place" (p. 24). This dilemma is continually brought to my attention as I talk to superintendents of schools about their relationships with school boards. "Why is it that you have such a good relationship with your board?" I ask. "We had an agreement from the beginning that there would be no surprises," they respond. "When do you learn the most?" I then ask. "When there are surprises," they answer. The superintendent's roles as politician and learner are often contradictory.

A major result of the scholarship of many hermeneutic thinkers is emphasis on the student (including the student of curriculum planning) as a creator, not just a consumer, of curriculum. Maxine Greene (1975), for example, writes about the networks of relationships that all curriculum planners create. The idea of networking (network creating) sees the person as having internal authority to stretch informally in many and diverse directions that are not predetermined. As a result, the networker increases his or her sense of efficacy.

What are the practical implications of hermeneutic theory for curriculum leadership and planning? The following description of a curriculum project will help us answer this question.

John was clear as to his goals for involvement in the Stone Street Project at the onset. These goals fit with the project goals: (a) to systematically build a knowledge base focusing on bureaucratic and professional forces exerted on decision makers in all similar organizations; (b) to weigh the extent to which decision makers can and should operate in the professional decision-making mode in the area of curriculum and instruction, while at the same time operating most effectively in the bureaucratic mode in noncurriculum and instruction (governance) matters; and (c) to disseminate findings, with special attention given to what might and might not be useful to other leaders in similar settings.

John felt that these understandings might lead to strategies for change in the setting being studied, but this wasn't his main interest. In fact, in his own mind, John thought that understandings achieved might well lead to the development of strategies for change that would be initiated in another setting at another time.

Those who advocate understanding as a primary interest of curriculum planners have been criticized in many ways, including the following:

1. Philosophical analysis and criticism can lead to understanding, but equal attention should be given to the implementation of such understanding in settings. Hermeneutics theory stands back and tries to objectify too much (Macdonald, 1980, p. 5).

2. Understanding as a primary interest of curriculum planners is not in step with our culture's scientific and technical way of viewing things. It is therefore of little practical use. Because most of our society's organizations are highly bureaucratic, hermeneutic theory simply doesn't prepare persons for their roles in such organizations.

The third conception of curriculum leadership and planning is based on the assumption that *praxis* (reflective action) has the potential "for emancipating human beings from unnecessary social constraints on their freedom" (Macdonald, 1980, p. 5). Curriculum planners who are primarily interested in liberation give attention to "the forming of social relations, rewards, and learning expectations in curriculum by economic and occupational interest structures, social class and power structure, and the use of language as distorted by work and power arrangements, as well as the form of language itself" (Macdonald, 1980, p. 6).

Critical theorists of this persuasion recognize the role that control and understanding must play in curriculum planning, but they want to take a third step. It is their emphasis on self-reflection through praxis that bonds these scholars together.

What is it that the curriculum planner must do? The curriculum planner must (a) identify and understand ways in which persons are dominated or constrained, (b) know what potentialities can be emancipated or liberated, and (c) guide progressive social development (Macdonald, 1980).

The following case illustrates a curriculum planner engaged in the liberation frame of mind:

> Jamie was a student of her culture and society as well as a student of other cultures and societies. She was especially concerned that our society has given a good deal of attention to the psychology of the person but little attention to the psychology of organizations. She believed her role as a curriculum planner included giving attention to this societal reality.
>
> When Jamie entered into the alliance with other curriculum leaders, she wanted to know if they shared her concern for the psychology of organizations. Most did, which was enough to spur Jamie on to formulate a project. As the curriculum-planning group began to get the project off the ground, Jamie reminded them that changes aimed at the person were misdirected, for a changed person could reenter an organization and be absorbed or co-opted by the organization itself. She therefore argued that the curriculum leadership team should give most of its attention to making organizational changes from which personal changes would evolve. For example, she felt that there should always be at least two educators from a school system in attendance at conferences and meetings. In this way they would have a support group in their home school settings.
>
> At the same time, Jamie emphasized the role of self-reflection on the part of persons, especially the core group of leaders in the project.

Criticism of the liberation point of view has come from many quarters. The following is a summary of some of this criticism.

1. Bureaucratic structures in our society simply will not tolerate moving beyond understanding to action. The fabric of our society will not take the pushing and shoving that we endured in the 1960s.

2. We are so locked into technical processes in our society that liberation processes will not fit. The person who practices liberation and emancipation will surely be a social misfit.

3. Few leaders are capable of integrating theory and practice. Praxis—reflective action—is an ideal that is too demanding in the real world.

In this section of the chapter, I have demonstrated that the curriculum leader's conception of curriculum planning influences his or her curriculum-planning behaviors. Both behaviors and conceptions are based on a foundation or substructure we identified as basic assumptions.

THE OUTER CURRICULUM
AND THE INNER CURRICULUM

The control orientation of the curriculum leader, in the culture of curriculum as a course of study, rests on the assumption that authority is located outside the learner (student and teacher) in textbooks, curriculum guides, and courses of study. This is why we refer to it as the *outer curriculum*. Transmission of knowledge, part of the mimetic tradition, is the goal (Jackson, 1986). (The Greek word *mimetes* means imitator.) The key question raised by followers of the mimetic tradition is this: What knowledge is of most worth?

Because authority is located in textbooks, curriculum guides, and the like, teachers can easily assign blame to someone above them in the hierarchy: They wrote a poor textbook. The curriculum guide is inadequate. The principal told me I had to do it this way. Teachers know that authority for the curriculum is located in administrators' interpretations of written materials, but teachers often misinterpret and sometimes don't even know the content of written materials. For example, teachers in a leadership seminar were asked if a sense of mission was important in their school system. A participant excitedly raised her hand. "We had a nationally known consultant work with us on a mission statement." "What is your mission?" she was asked. "I don't know," she replied. "It's back at my school in a notebook."

There is a hierarchy of subject matter in the culture of curriculum as a course of study. Grades for some courses don't count when colleges and universities compute a prospective student's grade-point average. In effect, band, orchestra, dance, art, and some other subjects are considered *extra*curricular. This fits with the age-old conception that people who work with their hands don't use their heads. The "some animals are more equal than others" philosophy is also expressed when students who take advanced academic subjects receive bonus points that increase their grade-point averages.

The culture of curriculum as a course of study has a left-brain orientation; the self is seen as a subset of the world (Bogen, 1979). The learner's experiences take a backseat to external authorities. Curriculum as a course of study is always reactive, never proactive. You will read about future curriculum topics in the editorial pages of newspapers. In short, teachers are curriculum implementers (reactors) not curriculum makers (actors). Infantilization of schools, schooling, and teachers can result from the bureaucratization of curriculum as a course of study. Teachers are treated like children rather than professionals.

The culture of the *inner curriculum*, what each person experiences as learning settings are cooperatively created, has a very different orientation. Consider briefly what these people have in common:

- A custodian with a special interest in wildflowers leads a middle-school class on a nature-trail walk, with the teacher at the end of the line of students.
- An assistant principal in a high school makes a point of being in the company of a student who was disciplined

the previous day, so that the student will continue to feel accepted.

- An elementary school principal eats breakfast once a week with bus drivers and emphasizes their special role in reaching children.
- A teacher engaged in lunchroom supervision teaches table manners to socially unschooled children.

The teachers and principals in these situations believe that curriculum as a course of study is simply a springboard for inner curriculum, what each person experiences as learning settings are cooperatively created (Brubaker, 1982a). (Imagine the outer curriculum as a rectangle within inner curriculum, which is the shape of an amoeba. Curriculum as a course of study is something to react to as persons grow, learn, and change.)

The primary role of experience in the inner curriculum places this way of viewing teaching and learning in the ontological realm. That is, one's being (who one is) is more important than what one does (Tillich, 1952). (The person's inner thoughts, basic assumptions about reality, and intentions will not always be visible in one's behavior.) As stated in the introduction to Part I, "The Meaning of Curriculum," a major question raised by those interested in the inner curriculum is "How shall I live with myself?" The challenge is to be autobiographical without being narcissistic. A second major question is "How shall we live together?" Interaction between the self and others in community is a natural area of study for the curriculum scholar.

The inner curriculum rests firmly in the transformative rather than the mimetic tradition (Jackson, 1986). The teacher and students are learners who are expected to experience a qualitative change, often of dramatic proportion—a metamorphosis, so to speak (Jackson, 1986, pp. 120–121). As Jackson has clearly stated, authority is located in the person's search for understanding and liberation; as a result of this search, something within the learner, his or her essence, changes (Jackson, 1986).

The masculine effort to take charge and to control what we found in the tradition of curriculum as a course of study now incorporates the feminine intuitive, artistic role. There is an element of control within understanding and liberation, but control is clearly not the dominant interest of the person oriented to the culture of the inner curriculum (Habermas, 1971).

Those who commit themselves to the inner curriculum make themselves vulnerable in ways that outer curriculum advocates do not. Contradictions, paradoxes, and dilemmas are grist for the inner curriculum person's inquiry. Single causation is replaced by multiple causation and, at times, no known causation. Mystery can play an important heuristic role. Chance and serendipity are often entertained as part of artists' common bond—an interest in quality rather than quantity. (Can you imagine a case being made that Renoir was a better painter than another artist because his canvases were larger or that he painted more of them?)

The educator with an inner curriculum orientation knows that the setting of ends, activity selection, and evaluation are often simultaneous processes rather than part of a linear, sequential formula. Goals, intentions of a general nature, open up new vistas for exploration. Behavioral objectives too often constrict the learner, thereby treating him or her as a passive vessel rather than as an active learner. Goal-free evaluation can play an important role because it stimulates the learner's involvement in creative activities without constraining him or her to predetermined ends.

Because authority is located in the learner's search for understanding and liberation, he or she is responsible for decisions made during the search. Collegiality, rather than hierarchical command-down decision making, means that the educator oriented to the inner curriculum can't blame higher-ups for difficulties in the system. Advocates of the inner curriculum are encouraged to be proactive rather than simply reactive. Inner curriculum is lived. Outer curriculum is taken. We create each other and ourselves in the formation of community as advocates of the inner curriculum.

The culture of the inner curriculum is primarily right-brain oriented, with the world seen as a subset of the self (Bogen, 1979). Or, as Emerson said, "Every mind must know the whole lesson for itself" (1903, p. 10). A superintendent of schools, who is committed to the inner curriculum, describes the difference this view of curriculum made in his leadership:

> Two themes are central to me as a superintendent of schools: empowerment and the improvement of services. The traditional top-down compliance system approach to leadership simply doesn't work. It takes too much time to micromanage people, and this way of doing things denies people ownership. People sit around waiting for the next order and can always blame someone higher up, rather than accepting responsibility for their work. Our greatest asset is the minds and souls of adults expected to give services to students. When they feel they have authority over the work they do, the result is greater self-understanding, productivity, and higher morale. The inside-out definition of the inner curriculum helps each person find authority in himself or herself and emphasizes cooperation and teamwork as we create learning environments for all interested in schools—children and adults.
>
> One example illustrates what I've done to support the inner curriculum of principals. I inherited a checklist system for evaluating principals. I continued to use the checklist for a couple of years because principals were used to it, but I added a section that was a handwritten profile of each principal's leadership. Principals were also asked for their own self-portrait of their leadership. The sharing of these subjective accounts is all that counts now with the principals. We've simply eliminated the checklists.

What the superintendent of schools has done in reality is to invite principals and others to be human and authentic.

CONCLUSION

Curriculum as a course of study, and curriculum as what each person experiences as learning settings are cooperatively created, are human inventions (definitions) that serve as a major tool by which one creates environments that later shape and influence one's own behavior (Yinger, 1978). In effect, each definition is persuasive and evaluative, for it is an attempt to alter attitudes in a desired direction. This is the challenge facing curriculum leaders, one that we should all view as an invitation to learning and action. In Part II of this book, we will see how one's vocation or calling influences his or her desire to be with students and colleagues, and we will treat the important matter of continuing to want to be there, or avoiding burnout.

Case 2: You Are Asked for Your Definition of Curriculum at a Staff Development Retreat

You are a member of the leadership team in your school. This five-member group, consisting of three teachers, a parent, and the assistant principal, has planned an excellent conference (retreat) for faculty and five parents who represent the community. You look forward to the dialogue, good fellowship, food, and recreation.

The opening session consists of a guest speaker from the university, after which there will be five breakout groups that will react to the speaker's address. You and the other members of the curriculum council will give leadership to the breakout groups.

The speaker challenges the audience to define curriculum as what each person experiences as learning settings are cooperatively created, rather than simply as a course of study. The speaker adds that curriculum as a course of study should be the best it can be, but it is ultimately only a springboard for all of the learning experiences students and teachers acquire.

As the head of one of the five discussion groups, it is your responsibility to begin the discussion by giving your reaction to the speaker. What will you say? Please choose the best response from the alternatives that follow:

1. You disagree with the speaker. Curriculum has traditionally been defined as a course of study, and you believe that this is both necessary and sufficient.

2. You agree with the speaker. Support this innovative definition.

3. You state the position that the definition of curriculum is of little consequence.

Case 2: Rationales for the Alternative Responses

1. The speaker's message is troublesome. It provides each teacher with the license to go in any direction that he or she pleases. It ignores or minimizes the fact that there is an essential body of knowledge that all students must learn. State your case passionately and warn members of the group of impending chaos if the innovative definition of curriculum is adopted. The difficulty in this response is that it immediately locks you into the traditional without considering alternative responses. Please consider other possible reactions.

2. The speaker has delivered a powerful and important message. Each person's experiences are central to curriculum. This definition includes students and teachers. Curriculum is indeed a springboard that must be revised to meet new societal and school needs. This is a good choice; lead the discussion in your group to the application of the innovative definition of curriculum to school settings. The curriculum council will have an important role to play in reviewing and revising curriculum as a course of study. The principal and assistant principal will need to understand that they are catalysts and coordinators rather than directors.

3. One's definition of curriculum is of little consequence compared with one's actions as a curriculum leader. Theory is a smokescreen that takes educators' attention away from practice. Although there is some truth in this argument, one's definition of curriculum can be a map for creative curriculum leaders. Leaders who deny the value of defining curriculum may well be viewed as cynics. At the very least, they lose the opportunity to establish an affinity with those who want an operating definition of curriculum. Choose a better response.

Case 3: PTA Speaker Endorses National Curriculum Standards

The president of your school's Parent Teacher Association is a professor from a nearby university. The PTA president has invited a nationally recognized education expert to speak at the fall meeting. You are invited to respond to the speaker's address because of your leadership and speaking ability.

A large turnout is present for the address, and the speaker delivers a dynamic and often humorous lecture. She argues that national education policy has been set for the next four to eight years, and at the head of the list is the need for national education standards, national curriculum frameworks, and a national examination system. She adds that the national examinations will tell us how curriculum is operationally defined. Evaluation of students will include performance assessment, projects, and portfolios. The speaker concludes by saying that we will have to live with a paradox: a national orientation to education that is local in implementation. Teachers must serve as coaches who will help students "beat" the Educational Testing Service in much the same way that advanced placement teachers currently try to beat the test makers. Teachers who are up to it will be inventive brokers who relate to the national-local paradox. Such teachers will do extraordinary work to reach and surpass national standards. Competition will be the driving force that will elicit the best in teachers and students. When the system is working correctly, it will look much like architectural competition. All competitors must meet building codes, but creativity will bloom.

It is now time for your reaction to the speech. What will you say? Please choose the best response from the alternatives that follow:

1. The price for following the speaker's advice is simply too high. State your case for this position.

2. The speaker is on target. Support the speaker's position with all of the expertise you have.

3. This is a nonissue. Explain why.

Case 3: Rationales for the Alternative Responses

1. The idea of a national curriculum with a national examination system is a serious mistake. Each student is unique and should be challenged to use his or her talents to the best of his or her ability. The speaker's position, if implemented, would sort students into winners and losers. It is an antidemocratic position. In fact, the national testing and curriculum

movement creates large bureaucracies that further inhibit teachers, thus sapping their creativity.

2. The speaker is on target. We must have high expectations for all children. We have made education so unresponsive to the individual that we have neglected standards. In fact, the speaker's position is very democratic because it is a pathway to equal opportunity for all who work hard. Therefore, a democracy based on merit can finally be achieved in our country. All children will benefit. Furthermore, competition is at the heart of our social structure. Students need to learn to compete in order to survive in our culture. In relating to this position favorable to the speaker's thesis, the educator must simply ask if the benefits outweigh the costs. My position is that they don't and the cost is primarily focused on the teacher's professional judgment and creativity. In fact, many bureaucratic measures designed to eliminate teachers who are considered "bad apples" fail to rid the profession of incompetents, while at the same time curtailing the creative efforts of exemplary teachers.

3. It certainly gets one's attention to say that this is a nonissue. The difficulty is that the issue simply won't go away by calling it a nonissue. The movement toward national testing and curriculum is very much with us today.

PART II

Education as Vocation: How a "Sense of Calling" Influences Curriculum Development

In Part I, "The Meaning of Curriculum," we saw that the inner curriculum (what each person experiences as learning settings are cooperatively created) and the outer curriculum (course of study) are interactive and interdependent. In Part II, we attend to the creative curriculum leader's view of vocation. We commonly think of one's vocation as his or her job or career, but the Latin verb *vocare*, to call, has a much deeper and comprehensive meaning particularly with respect to those who enter the field of education.

Some educators have had a sense of destiny with regard to teaching from the time they were little children (Peck, 1993). An educator in the Midwest talks about her sense of destiny:

> My kindergarten teacher and I had the same last name, and so when I played school in the neighborhood, I was usually chosen to be the teacher. After school and during the summertime, my friends and I went to the playground and I was usually the teacher during recess time. I knew that I wanted to be a teacher from the time I was five. In fact, I wanted to be one of the best, just like my best teachers.

An interesting thing about the feeling that you are called to do great things is that your calling "will likely be worked out in ways that you currently can't even begin to imagine" (Peck, 1993, p. 70). The Midwestern educator continues her story:

> My career path is a real mystery to me. After teaching for ten years, I became interested in special education because of a special child in my classroom whom I didn't think I was reaching. I returned to school, got my master's degree in special education, and became a special education teacher. Then I was asked to become director of special education in the school system. This led me to a doctoral program with a major in special education. A year ago, a friend at the university started a special education program for preschool children and asked me to follow her as the director of the program. I had no idea at age five that I would be involved in so many different things, but I still have the same love for children that I had when I was a child.

It is with regard to the educator's love for children and desire to be helpful that participants in creative curriculum leadership seminars have had the most provocative discussions. As one participant commented, "The bottom line for me as an educator is that I have always wanted to be helpful. In fact, in talking to my friends, we have agreed that we often play the martyr role." She continued,

In what other profession do you want to go to the bathroom but can't? I developed the martyr role so well that at times I felt that I shouldn't get anything out of teaching. I asked myself, "Why?" I finally concluded that when I don't play the martyr role, I show my vulnerability and others have a string to pull. They can control me and, more than anything else, I wanted to control others as a helpful rescuer.

A special education teacher added, "There is a whole new world out there for exceptional children now, and I want to give children the same rights as other children have. My challenge is to be an advocate who cares rather than a caretaker who does for, rather than with, special children."

A third educator said, "I not only wanted to control students by being a rescuer but I wanted to fix their problems quickly. In the process, I thought things were my problems that weren't."

A colleague in school administration introduced another dimension to the discussion:

I had my own vision as to what education should be and discovered as a teacher I had little power. I moved into administration to get that power and do good things for children. [She added,] One thing that motivated me to move into administration was that I didn't like what most school administrators did with power.

A seminar participant captured the zeitgeist (feeling in the air) of our discussion: You know, you really have to have your head on straight in relating to your vocation.

In Chapter 3, "Learning From Your Professional Autobiography," I discuss those influences that have shaped one's sense of calling, or vocation. The talents you have developed were probably sharpened by comments from parents, teachers, scout leaders, coaches, friends, and others in the community. We explore these comments and the decisions you have made within their context. In some cases, you have accepted such influences; in other cases you have decided to move in new directions.

Chapter 4, "Looking Forward to Work: The Power of Wanting to Be There," discusses a source of power available to you that has received little attention in education literature: your desire to do what you do at work. Nobody always wants to go to work or always likes work, but if you consistently enjoy the core of your work, there is a much greater chance that you will be successful at what you do.

Chapter 5, "Keeping the Fire in Your Vocation," focuses on how experienced educators fight burnout and boredom. They have learned to find ways in which they can continue to be motivated to be creative curriculum leaders.

In this section of the book, we see that each person is both unique and precious. "We have it within our power to change our nature when we need to" (Peck, 1993, p. 82). Another way to say this is that each of us writes his or her life script.

It should be added that creative curriculum leaders exist within particular cultures of organizations, and these cultures may vary considerably (Peck, 1993). We are therefore confronted with the question, "How do we decide what kind of culture we are called to?" (Peck, 1993, p. 238). This question speaks to one's comfort and vision with regard to where power is located and how it is exercised. This matter is addressed in the chapters that follow.

3

Learning From Your Professional Autobiography

Each of us has an inner child of the past living within us. Those who needed to build no walls have access to that child's creativity and spontaneity. Those who had to leave this crucial core behind can tear down the walls, see what the child needed but didn't have, and begin to provide it now.

—Gloria Steinem (1992, pp. 38–39)

Your sense of calling, or vocation, is an inner voice that gives you direction in your educational profession and indeed in life itself. Before we look at those factors that have shaped your life and vocation, let us examine those vital forces that may serve you in doing autobiography.

The first force that helps involve us in telling our story and being a creative curriculum leader is recognizing that *one is always a choice maker*. Some contemporary psychiatrists and psychologists have made an important contribution in helping us see that we are not victims of others' decisions. Rather, we always have the power to make decisions that influence ourselves, others, and the environment. Let us examine an extreme case to illustrate the power we always have as choice makers. Imagine for a moment that my bureaucratic superior is dissatisfied with my work and therefore decides to fire me. If I were in the victim frame of mind, I might well tell you, "My boss fired me," after which I would say things to get your support and sympathy for me as a victim of another person's whims. I might also say that the situation in which I worked was impossible, and I just couldn't do anything about it. If, on the other hand, I recognize that I always have the power to make decisions, I might say to you, "My boss fired me, and I've decided to respond to this by doing thus and so." In this latter case, I wouldn't play innocent by pretending that I have no power to respond to the boss's action (May, 1972). There is a world of difference between these two frames of mind, and this difference can be seen in the attitudes and behaviors of educators. The following expressions and phrases reflect differences between the victim and the nonvictim:

Victim	Nonvictim
I can't do anything as long as this person is boss.	I can't do everything I want to do while this person is boss, but I can do some things that are important to me.
Nothing I do will make a difference.	I can make a difference.
What's the use?	What I do is important.

The nonvictim way of thinking is not meant to discount the very real pain and suffering that occur in the world today. Nor is it meant as a rationale for not helping those who are in trouble. It does say that those in dire straits cannot begin to help themselves out of such difficulty until they realize that they are choice makers.

The view that a person always has choices has a rich tradition in literature. John Steinbeck uses this view as the theme and thesis for *East of Eden* (1952). Lee, the Chinese servant of Adam Trask, shares with Adam the secret that he has spent ten years trying to understand a brief part of the Cain and Abel story in Genesis. It is the part where Jehovah asks Cain why he is so angry. Jehovah says, "If thou doest well, shalt thou not be accepted? And if thou doest not well, sin lieth at the door. And unto thee shall be his desire, and *thou shalt* rule over him" (emphasis added). It was the *thou shalt* part that troubled Lee, for it was God's promise that Cain could conquer sin. For two years, Lee went to nearby San Francisco to study with learned Chinese scholars about this passage in Genesis. These scholars invited a learned rabbi to study with them. Together they discovered that the Hebrew word *timshel* should be interpreted thou mayest, which also led them to the conclusion that thou mayest not. Lee discovered that *persons always have a choice.*

A second force that gives vitality to the creative curriculum leader and autobiographer is *intentionality.* Paul Tillich (1952), noted theologian and philosopher, argued that "man's vitality is as great as his intentionality" (pp. 81–82). Our intentions naturally flow from our sense of efficacy: "I can make a difference" becomes "I will make a difference by doing thus and so."

A third force evolves from a *sense of efficacy and intentionality.* It is the power of a dream of what is desirable and possible to accomplish. Knowing that I can make a difference, and intending to do good things, must be followed by a dream or vision of what is desirable and possible to accomplish. This dream is often painted with broad brush strokes rather than fine, detailed lines. The dream begins with "I wonder if . . ."

(See Chapter 6, "Creative Curriculum Leadership in Practice," for a more detailed discussion of personal and organizational vision.)

WHAT CAN I LEARN FROM MY PROFESSIONAL AUTOBIOGRAPHY?

The challenge is to think through and then express the patterns and principles that have been operative in one's educational experience (Pinar, 1975). In the process, the creative curriculum leader as autobiographer generally will achieve a deeper self-understanding. In listening to others relate their professional autobiographies, he or she will begin to arrive at an understanding of patterns of influences on decision makers, as realized in their behavior (Pinar, 1975). The special benefit to women and persons in other marginalized groups is cited by Gloria Steinem (1992): "I combined this research [on the factors that affect self-esteem] with women's personal stories, which are, like all personal accounts of any group that has been marginalized, our best textbooks: the only way to make our experience central" (p. 4).

Where do curriculum leaders start in order to use their autobiographies to make sense of their professional decision-making styles? William Pinar, curriculum theorist, suggests that we begin with free-flowing associative forms of thinking. The following serves as an example:

> I really enjoy trying to make sense out of what goes on in schools and I try to do this in a systematic way. . . . Where did I get this interest? My father was a fantastic bridge player and worker of crossword puzzles. . . . I think this helped me respect the mind and the exercise of intelligence. . . . I have a real concern for the person as a learner and I am interested in the social forces that influence the person. . . . Where does this come from? . . . I grew up in a small town in Wisconsin which gave me a sense of community. . . . The fact that this town was located in Wisconsin's liberal atmosphere was also a factor. . . . And, my mother had a real moral sense in that she believed that some things were ethically just and good. She dinged away at that. (Macdonald, 1977)

Critical incidents in one's life, often related to one's professional life, can precipitate hard psychological work. One good way to do this work is by writing a story of what happened to you and the sense you made of this critical incident. You may or may not wish to share your writing with a trusted friend. The following educator's story illustrates story writing:

A few days ago I woke up in a cold sweat. "What is the problem?" I said to myself and then to my wife. After brainstorming a bit, it was clear that I dreaded going to a meeting largely because I was going to be the only person of my gender there. Why did this bother me? The committee was charged with hearing the grievance of a faculty member against the department chair. Both were also of the other, rather than my, gender. Why was this gender issue important to me? Discussion with my wife helped me see that I placed myself in the rescuer role. I hated hearing the voice of judgment I associated with my father, the voice I was charged with invoking as a committee member, and my way of coping with voice of judgment was the same one I acted out as a child: I tried to rescue my mother from my father. I felt intense pressure to rescue the aggrieved woman faculty member from the voice of judgment. I had identified the silent assumption underlying my stress. This understanding lifted the dark cloud overhead and I went to the meeting and played the role of another committee member rather than the rescuer.

Curriculum students often find it difficult to construct professional autobiographies. They have said things such as, "We aren't used to giving our opinions because our teachers, especially in college, always wanted us to be objective. This seems so subjective. Our professors taught us to be scientific, and this doesn't seem very scientific." Always locating power in others can make one empathy-sick. Gloria Steinem (1992) describes how this happened to her:

> I finally began to admit that I, too, was more aware of other people's feelings than my own; that I had been repeating the patterns of my childhood without recognizing them . . . and in short, my childhood years—a part of my life I thought I had walled off—were still shaping the present as surely as a concealed magnet shapes metal dust. (p. 7)

Proponents of the autobiographical method recognize the rich source of ideas and feelings within each of us. Furthermore, the many and diverse ways of looking at life around us are a reality to those who hold them. A simple example will illustrate how perceptions of an event, the opening of summer school in a university, vary:

> In walking to my office at the university today, two weeks prior to the official opening of summer school, I stopped to talk to the men who were putting asphalt on the student parking lot. One man remarked, "We won't be able to start summer school on time since the parking lot won't be ready." A similar attitude prevailed at the bookstore, where the aisles were filled with boxes of books ready to be opened and shelved. A clerk said, "We've never been so far behind." Workers in the central administration building had a different view as they registered students and collected tuition money with the knowledge that summer school would indeed start on time.

Participants in the creative curriculum leadership process can simply be expected to have differing perceptions of events. These perceptions are formed in part by their personal histories, which is basically the argument for giving attention to such autobiographies. As we participate in the process of sharing autobiographies, we begin to attain a *reciprocity of perspectives*. Out of our subjective perspectives emerge rationality and meaning, for perspectives blend and perceptions confirm each other.

BEGINNING TO DO AN AUTOBIOGRAPHY

As you complete the talent inventory on page 41, you will flesh out a portrait of your calling, or vocation. During a typical day at work, you will use more talents than you probably realize you have. Your first task is to write in the left column a chronology of an ideal (best) school-year day. Please do this from the time you get up in the morning until the time you go to sleep at night. The first item or two may read something like this: 6 A.M.: got up; 6:15 A.M.: showered and put on favorite clothes; 6:30: ate a good breakfast; and so on. Your second task is to list in the second column the unique qualities (talents) you used in correspondence with the times you listed in the first column. Each of these qualities is a tape that goes off in your head when you encounter a particular situation. For example, 8:15 A.M.: I used my organizational skills to introduce a new lesson. Your third task is to name, in the third column, the sources of the tape you listed in the second column. These sources may include a parent or parents, a teacher, a religious figure, an aunt, an uncle, a grandparent, a friend, or others. For example, 9 A.M.: I took the students to the media center and introduced them to basic computer skills for finding materials. My aunt, an alumnus of the college I attended, introduced me to the college by taking me to its library. I've loved libraries and media centers ever since.

Your final task is to write in the fourth column your decision either to keep and act out the tape from childhood, or reverse the tape and not act it out as you were instructed to as a child. For example, 2 P.M.: I used my intelligence and physical bearing to break up a fight at school. The tape that went off in my head was to get away from the fight. That's what my parents, teachers, and other adults taught me. But I then reversed the tape, because I knew that in my role as teacher, I had to address the matter rather than walk away from it.

Hundreds of educators have responded to this talent inventory. Some of the talents they have listed are preparation skills; organizational skills; proactivity; follow-through; the ability to be articulate, verbally and in writing; a sense of humor; the ability to motivate others to work together on committees; being a good team member; and being firm but fair with students.

One of the main findings of educators in completing the talent inventory is the seemingly endless array of contradictions that face them (Brubaker & Simon, 1993). That is, they are expected to somehow reconcile opposing or mixed messages. After reading the following list of contradictions, educators were asked to create metaphors that best describe their reactions to the list. They responded, "I sometimes feel like I'm herding cats." "I feel like a juggler." "It's like steering a dog by moving its tail." The somewhat general contradictions they listed were as follows:

Professional autonomy but state regulation and supervision

Told that we are professionals with expertise, but outside consultants are the experts

Competition with other schools, but cooperation with other schools expected

Display accomplishments, but quietly go about your business

Think (plan) ahead, but catch up (look backward)

Be positive, but face the negative

It is clear from educators' responses to this exercise that contradictions are double-edged. They are often a source of consternation while at the same time a challenge that can bring out our creativity as educators. How is this possible? Contradictions produce interior tension that awakens us from comfortable routines, traditions, and rituals. "There is a constant battle in each of us," according to psychiatrist Arnold A. Hutschnecker (1974), "between the forces of excitation and inhibition"(p. 8). In fact, it is the contradictions that really bother us that force us to be proactive as creative curriculum leaders. There is always an element of anxiety in this proactivity. The role of anxiety in creativity has been recognized by artists throughout the ages. Michelangelo's paintings of human beings have distended or dilated eyes, a telltale sign of anxiety (May, 1975).

Some contradictions call for hard psychological work. Others are a cause for celebration, even though they also require different kinds of work, usually of a more technical, logistical nature. For example, Janet and Jim are bright students who recently joined your class. You enjoy their creative insights, but they are so quick that you find it hard work to create challenging assignments for them while other students plod along. The payoff for you is that you learn more as a teacher because of this challenge, and so do other students in the class.

Or, take the instance of a principal in a large middle school. Two faculty members are particularly bright, forthright, and outspoken. One, George, is referred to by colleagues as the "Minister of Responsible Disturbance." It would be much easier to lead faculty meetings if these two faculty members were not there. At the same time, faculty meetings are more interesting and decisions are usually better because of their presence.

A TALENT INVENTORY

Chronology of an Ideal (Best) School-Year Day	My Unique Qualities In This Day (Tapes)	Sources of These Tapes	Personal Decisions to Keep These Tapes (Act on Them)

Purpose Statement: My purpose is to use my talents of _____, and _____ to support and inspire others to identify and use their talents.

CREATIVE LEADERSHIP = USING MY TALENTS TO HELP OTHERS IDENTIFY AND USE THEIR TALENTS.

Some of the more bothersome contradictions facing educators are political and financial, including the following:

1. Our school's children are getting higher test scores, which pleases the parents and board of education, but are they really learning more or learning what is important to learn?

2. The board of education and superintendent constantly talk about the lack of financial resources but then hire consultants whose contribution is questionable.

3. When students in special situations achieve, we lose federal funds.

4. Many teachers won't stay after school to hand out report cards, but they say they really care about children.

5. The best teachers are rewarded with jobs in the central office.

6. They talk about teamwork in this school, but the most prestigious honor is a solitary one: Teacher of the Year.

7. Boards of education choose leaders they think they can control.

8. Because of questionable teacher-evaluation procedures, poor teachers survive.

9. Board members talk about hiring the best persons for jobs but pressure us to nominate their own favorites for positions.

10. Board members and administrators talk about excellence, but those who suck up prosper.

Occasionally, a contradiction comes home in our personal lives, and our rhetoric sounds hollow because of inconsistent actions. A teacher of learning disabled (LD) students describes this experience: "I have always been a strong advocate for my LD students, and my daughter has respected me for this. However, I was aghast when my daughter wanted to date one of my LD students. I objected, and my daughter said, 'Mom, you're a hypocrite." This brings us to one of the most important questions facing the educational leader: "Whose ox is being gored?"

Please take a moment to identify in the chart that follows those contradictions you expect to celebrate (or do celebrate) as a teacher and those contradictions you expect will (or currently do) demand hard psychological work. Then look at the following responses from other educators to this assignment.

Column 1 (Celebrate)	Column 2 (Reconcile)

Column 1 (Celebrate)	Column 2 (Reconcile)
We have excellent parent involvement, and this means we give many of our resources (e.g., time and effort) to parents.	I always feel like I'm the person in the middle.
There are always more desires than resources, something I celebrate because we want people to be proactive.	I appreciate the energy of young staff members, but many are really naïve about what I, an experienced educator, can do.
I appreciate honest, helpful advice.	Some teachers nag, which I don't like, and yet I admire commitment.
Because I have a proven track record, they call on me to do more than I sometimes want to do.	As a female educator, I always confront (have to deal with) the "old boys" club.

Although it is not always easy to do, it is good to remind ourselves that there is no movement without friction, and difficult contradictions provide such friction. They challenge us to learn more about ourselves from our interactions with others and the environment.

CONCLUSION

Doing one's professional autobiography and then sharing autobiographies with others can be one of the most rewarding experiences the creative curriculum leader can have. We get to know ourselves and others better—an important step in the creation of community. We can see what those special talents are that give us a sense of vocation or calling.

Case 4: Personal Disclosure and the Leader's Credibility

You are at a seminar on curriculum leadership. There is a spirited discussion concerning whether leaders in an organization should deliberately create distance between self and others. One leader in your seminar presents a point of view with considerable forcefulness:

> At the beginning of his administration, President Clinton took a select group of advisers to Camp David for a weekend retreat. The press reported that a facilitator was working with the group at this retreat. President Clinton said that as a child he was called "chubby," and this negative labeling was very hurtful to him.
>
> This is the kind of thing that demeans the office of the presidency. The head of an organization not only represents self but also the institution of the presidency. You have to keep distance between yourself and others, and this kind of behavior by the president works against the credibility of the president and the institution of the presidency.

Another leader at the seminar strongly disagrees with the first leader's statement: "I have even greater respect for former

President Clinton because of this. He has demonstrated that he is human and at times suffers just like the rest of us."

You are asked for your views on this matter. What will you say, and what is the rationale for your position? Please choose from the alternative rationales that follow:

1. The first speaker's position is correct. Distance must be kept between the leader and others in the organization.

2. The second speaker is correct and the first speaker is off base. Showing your feelings and being close to followers is simply being human.

Case 4: Rationales for the Alternative Responses

1. Former President Clinton made a mistake in supporting a format with a facilitator. As president of the United States, he is the "boss," and he demeaned himself by stepping away from hierarchy. He should share such feelings in the privacy of his family but not outside of that institution. Some people will always take advantage of you if you let down your guard. Showing your emotions, particularly as a leader, scares a lot of people. Clinton added to people's fright by doing what he did. In summary, he made the mistake of stepping outside of his role.

2. This case is all about expectations—expectations one has of self and that others have of the leader. Former President Clinton's response was like a breath of fresh air. Most presidents have been out of touch with people and their own humanity. Clinton had a right to hurt, just like everybody else. Sharing his feelings about being wronged is a sign of good mental health, and his presidency is better because of such disclosure. He also broke the stereotype that only women are nurturing leaders. He exhibited real courage and leadership in what he did.

Case 5: Caring and Caretaking

An experienced educator who is nearing retirement gives a speech at a leadership seminar in your school system. The following are some of the educator's comments that were made in a sincere and informal manner:

One thing I learned early as a leader is that there are a lot of breakdowns. Relationships among teachers, teachers and students, teachers and administrators, teachers and parents, and teachers and central-office personnel sometimes break down.

For the first few years of my principalship, I fell into the trap of thinking that whenever something went wrong at school, it was my fault. For example, the superintendent visited our school when we had our annual carnival. A parent, who is also a friend of the superintendent, threw a soft-whip pie in the superintendent's face. I didn't know how the superintendent would react, and my immediate feeling was that I should have never let this happen. It's my fault that it happened. The fact that the superintendent was a good sport about this didn't eliminate my feeling.

After attending a workshop for principals on knowing thyself, I began to see that there is a difference between caring and caretaking. As the oldest child in the family, I was responsible for taking care of my younger brothers and sisters, and I carried this attitude of control and responsibility into college, teaching, and the principalship.

I simply wanted to tell you this story of my breakthrough because I couldn't begin to understand others and myself until I was willing to give up much of this control.

You have listened to this story. What thoughts do you have about it? Please choose from the following alternative responses:

1. As the principal, the person in charge of the school, you give up efforts to control things at your own peril. Be courteous to the speaker but remind yourself that the message just isn't one that will work for you.

2. The principal is a wise person. Take the principal's words to heart and map out ways in which you can apply them to your leadership position.

3. Ignore the message because it is basically irrelevant.

Case 5: Rationales for the Alternative Responses

1. The basic message of many religions is that one should always do for others. Trying to control school situations to prevent any problems from occurring is simply what a good leader does. For example, the principal is right for feeling guilty about what happened to the superintendent. If something goes wrong, prepare yourself for trouble, because you are accountable. The difficulty with this response and rationale is the high price you will pay for having it. You will constantly have to give resources to being on guard, and worrying can get you down. Search for a better response.

2. The basic question this wise educator speaks to is, "How shall I live with myself as well as others?" If you try to control everything, you will be codependent because you will take the blame for everything that happens. One of the first things you try to teach parents of special children, for example, is that they must encourage special children to take risks so that they learn to do as much as possible for themselves. This is the best answer, and the educator near retirement has given you good advice in an authentic way.

3. Staying out of it or hiding can save resources for you as a leader. The problem with this rationale is that the issue of caring and caretaking is at the core of the leadership issue. Find a better response that demonstrates a more professional and committed attitude.

4

Looking Forward to Work

The Power of Wanting to Be There

And if you sing though as angels, and love not the singing, you muffle man's ears to the voices of the day and the voices of the night.

—Kahlil Gibran (1923, p. 28)

A reading of students' professional autobiographies indicates that those who have a sense of calling and feel good about using their talents look forward to going to work each day. In being in touch with their histories, they feel that they can make a difference in the lives of their students. Although it simply makes sense that there's no substitute for wanting to be there, one discovers little research and writing on this subject (Brubaker, 1986).

The subject came to my attention when our family went to a restaurant. The hostess greeted us cordially and led us to our table, which was in an inviting setting.

Our waitress approached our table and said, "Can I help you," in a voice devoid of emotion. She wasn't unpleasant, and she wasn't pleasant. She was simply there. Our family reacted to her flattened affect by trying to pick up her spirits with humor and caring comments. No response. The result of this lack of interaction with the waitress, the leader who was expected to set the stage for a pleasant evening, was that the food was excellent but the dining experience was not. While riding home in the car, one of our children said, "The waitress acted as if she didn't want to be with us."

This experience stimulated my thinking about the importance of the leader sending a powerful message to followers: "I want to be with you." I suspect that each of us enters the work world daily asking questions such as, Does my boss think my contribution is special enough to want to be with me? Do my fellow workers value my work and want to be with me? If the answer is yes, the day seems a little shorter and the quality of work is better.

Teachers probably look to administrators, and children look to teachers, with the same question in mind: Do you want to be with me? When followers believe that the leader wants to be there with them, successful leadership is not necessarily assured; but, on the other hand, their belief that the leader *doesn't* want to be there certainly works against effective leadership.

With these thoughts in mind, I asked a Clemson University sophomore, who happened to be next to me on a flight from Greensboro to Boston, "How do you know during the first few minutes of a class whether the professor wants to be with you?" At first, she had difficulty with the question because she had naturally not prepared herself to answer such a different query. Once she got started, however, her answer was both clear and provocative:

> The first thing I look at is the way the professor walks into the classroom. Is he [for example] standoffish, or does he look at the students? If he looks at the class, and particularly if he has eye contact with each student, the professor has something at stake.
>
> Then I look to see if he expects us to work. There are several ways this is shown. Does he bring the textbook

with him? If he does, this demonstrates the important place the book will have in the course.

If the professor brings in the book, does he place it on the table with respect or does he toss it down as if it's not very important?

I also listen to the firmness of his voice. If his voice is firm, this is a first step in telling us that he has high expectations.

The professor's energy level tells me he is interested in me. He must have a high energy level and still seem reasonably relaxed. He uses this energy to set high expectations, but his being reasonably relaxed tells me he thinks I can meet these expectations.

I can tell almost immediately if the professor expects interaction between himself and the students, and among students. Does he expect us to be passive, or does he encourage us to ask real questions that don't have easy answers? And, does he listen to our answers, or is he so glued to his notes that he isn't interested in learning from us?

I'm really bothered if the professor immediately plays favorites. If he does he is probably there for social reasons and not the course itself. He wants our approval.

At the end of the conversation, this bright, articulate university student passionately delivered a postscript:

> You need to beware of something with us students. We need guidance, even to be told what to do at times, because we're scared of failure. The fewer decisions we make, the less risk of failure there is. Some of us are miserable and we see ourselves as victims because we see others having so much compared to us. You have a challenge with us: If you can, move us beyond these feelings to accept responsibility.

The conviction in the student's answer to my initial question said a great deal. She shared the simple but powerful truth that our enthusiasm for our work keeps us from becoming cynical—the deadliest of leadership qualities. A 19-year-old reminded me that as creative curriculum leaders, we have at our fingertips an obvious and often overlooked source of power—wanting to be there.

My conversation with this university student stimulated me to think more about leadership qualities that work for and against wanting to be there at work. The centerpiece for wanting to be there appears to be one's passion for learning. There seems to be a yearning on the part of educators to somehow recapture the curiosity, awe, wonder, and amazement we had when we started school. Adults have vivid memories of early discoveries. A principal in New Mexico said, "When I was a first grader, I saw leaves on trees. They were so green and I wondered where they came from and why they danced in the wind." Another educator added, "When I saw my first cater-pillar, I let it crawl up and down my arm. I was six."

Curiosity and a sense of exploration drive us forward and lead to new understandings. An experienced teacher from Arizona described her engagement in the creative process:

> When I was ten years old, we got our first television set from the Firestone Store, and we watched "I Love Lucy." I had my nose up to the screen, which taught my parents that I had eye trouble. I got glasses a week later. This made it possible for me to walk away from my mother in the grocery store—for the first time I could see.

Curiosity totally immerses a person in the joy of learning. Time and place take a backseat to the excitement of the moment. Listen to some more comments from adult educators who were asked to recall a childhood experience in which they were driven by a sense of exploration and a passion for learning:

> When I was seven or eight my Dad let me use his bamboo fishing pole. I could fish for myself. I caught and ate seventeen bluegills. The bobber kept going under. My brothers couldn't believe their sister caught all of these fish. Everybody said, "How wonderful!"

> I rode a train as a second grader. I had life space away from my family.

The first time I snorkeled, I was five years old. The bluefish kept touching me.

I remember the first day of school the sounds, smells, colors. The room was clean and neat.

I'll never forget the first day I learned to drive in the driveway. I was thirteen.

I remember listening to my cousin being born. I was six and stood outside and beneath the window. I saw my aunt with the baby on her lap. My aunt had a flat stomach again.

I rode an escalator in Birmingham when I was twelve. We had a one-story house in Enterprise, Alabama, and so this was a totally different experience for me.

I felt the warmth and saw the glow of a volcano thirty miles away. Where did everything go? I wondered . . .

When students were asked what characterized their being turned on to learning, where they experienced awe, wonder and amazement, they responded as follows:

A sense of humor

Risk taking, breaking routine, tradition, and ritual

Hope

A caring attitude toward self, others, and the challenge

Inner strength that comes from courage, commitment, and conviction

The feeling of being infected—totally absorbed

A sensitive attitude that allowed me to sense everything around me

The desire to do whatever I was doing well

The fact that I was prepared to learn—a matter of mind-set

Perseverance

The pure delight that comes from meeting the challenge

As creative curriculum leaders who are developing our own curricula, we face a question of great importance: How can I make a difference in the lives of others and myself, so that together we create environments that stimulate the qualities of exploration and learning listed here? Wanting to be there is a significant first step in realizing our vocation or calling. Continuing to want to be there or keeping the fire is the subject of the next chapter.

Case 6: Parent Contradicts Self in Speech to Faculty

You have been appointed as chair of the staff development committee. The parent of one of the students in your school is a prominent businessperson in your community and a dynamic speaker. You have invited him to speak to the faculty at the beginning of the year on the subject, "A Parent's View of School Reform."

The speaker begins with a brief sketch of his life, from its origins on a farm to his present position of prominence in his region of the country. He outlines the secret to success in general and his success in particular: (a) the ability to hustle—set goals and go after them; (b) perseverance; (c) people skills; and (d) excellent follow-through. He speaks with passion about how he graduated from the school of hard knocks, with his ability to draw from his many and diverse experiences as the main key to his success.

Then he moves to a critique of the schools. He argues that schools have neglected the basics of reading, writing, and mathematics. He elaborates by saying that schools should get rid of the frills and give attention only to the basic subjects.

Later in the day, your superintendent asks for your views on the speaker's presentation. The superintendent wasn't able to attend the speech. What will you say? Please choose the best of the following alternative responses:

1. The overall message communicated by the speaker verbally and nonverbally is that he has been successful because he has wanted to be there. People skills, hard work, setting goals, and follow-through are the keys to his passion for his work. This message is so strong and important that the

contradiction in relation to his expectations for curriculum is of little consequence. Relate the first part of his message to the superintendent as an example of the power of wanting to be there and leave it at that.

2. The first part of the speaker's message is correct, but he contradicts himself by advocating a view of curriculum that simply doesn't fit. Point this out to the superintendent but do so without being hypercritical.

3. Tell the superintendent that the speaker did a good job without referring to any specific content of the speech.

Case 6: Rationales for the Alternative Responses

1. The main part of the speaker's message is one that your superintendent can communicate to others even the speaker himself, if the superintendent talks to him. The difficulty with this response and rationale is that the superintendent won't have a sense of the total message of the speech if critics speak to the superintendent about the speech. Find a better response.

2. Your balanced description and critique of the speech will give the superintendent total context. The speaker's solution of returning to the basics contradicts his earlier remarks. Basic instruction emphasizes product (i.e., content) rather than process (such as goal setting). You might add that self-made businesspeople sometimes fail to see this contradiction. Your providing total context communicates trust in the superintendent's ability to use wisely the information that you provide. This is probably the best response.

3. A general surface view of the speech will keep you out of any controversy that the speech may have caused. Hiding can sometimes be wise. The problem with this response and rationale is that the superintendent can be blindsided by critics' comments with regard to the speech. You will come across to the superintendent, in this event, as a person with little expertise and conviction. In short, you won't appear to be a professional.

5

Keeping the Fire in Your Vocation

Arthur Ashe has always been a student of himself and his surroundings, a man engaged by the world, sure of himself.

—Frank Deford (1992, p. 62)

A sense of vocation or calling must be nurtured on a consistent basis. Such nurturing doesn't simply happen, but must be cultivated or sought out by the creative curriculum leader. As might be suspected, "Boredom is the deadliest poison, and this is a truism that it strikes hardest at the most comfortable" (Buckley, 1976, p. 26). Hard on the heels of boredom often comes cynicism, a deadly and cowardly form of superiority.

Proactive creative leadership is one antidote to boredom and cynicism, for it challenges us to use our talents to encourage others to do likewise. Creative leadership places us at the center of the action, for it helps us resolve the mental tug-of-war that each of us feels between two opposing forces: "Get involved!" versus "Hold back!" Those who opt for getting involved recognize that creative leadership can be a celebration of our ability to make a difference.

What are the steps one takes to meet this creative leadership challenge and keep the fire? First, in Chapter 3, "Learning From Your Professional Autobiography," we saw that it is helpful to ask the question, "What are my special talents?" Using one's talents is a matter of interest and proficiency. The possible distinction between interest and proficiency was brought to my attention by Gerald Austin, a National Football League referee and education consultant. As I left his office, I said to him, "How about you making the phone call to the superintendent of schools? I'm not good at that sort of thing." Gerald responded, "No, you're good at it, but you just don't especially enjoy doing it." He was right. I had little interest in or desire to make the call.

There can be a good deal of pressure associated with being expected to do well at something you're good at. For example, one of the reasons I enjoy the exercise of swimming so much is that I'm not expected to be good at it. It is simply a matter of swimming laps at my own speed, using an adequate but not outstanding swimming stroke. In playing tennis, however, there is often a certain kind of pressure associated with being good at it. I and others consider it to be "my sport."

It is important for the creative curriculum leader to remember the possible distinction between proficiency and interest in developing one's own curriculum, as well as curriculum as a course of study. Those we are expected to lead may want to try out various challenges, even though they don't feel especially comfortable or talented in each of these areas. Others may not want to use a particular talent, even though all within the setting know they are good at using it. This came to my attention in a school that was moving toward shared decision making. A teacher had recently moved into the system from Florida, where she had been a successful teacher and school leader. I assumed that she would welcome my invitation to serve as one of the grade-level leaders in the school. She looked at me with a somewhat pained expression and said, "I would rather not. My plate is full with other responsibilities, and I want to try out different challenges from those I met in my last school." "Fair enough," I responded, adding, "I appreciate your honest response and I respect the fact that you don't see yourself as a superwoman who has to say yes to every invitation."

The second step in meeting the leadership challenge and keeping the fire is demonstrated by the teacher who refused my invitation. She decided what she wanted to focus on to actively seek opportunities to improve the use of these talents. The mistake some people make is to ride off in all directions. This can lead to the feeling that they are doing nothing well. How do you prevent this? By identifying organizations and settings within organizations that are especially important to you.

The third step is a transitional one, moving from passive to active spectator. A university student described this transitional step: "I decided to sit in the 'T' in the front of the class and occasionally stop in to discuss matters of mutual interest with the professor." She added, "At first I thought of this as just 'sucking up' but the interesting thing I discovered is that professors are pretty lonely people who usually enjoy talking to students. And," she went on to say, "I took a new interest in the class because I had taken the initiative." Her activities had new focus and meaning, and she received a higher grade than she normally earned.

The fourth step the university student achieved was to identify leadership skills that stretched her to find new uses for her talents. Although she was nervous when she initiated contact with her professor, she learned that she possessed networking skills she didn't know she had. She was able to articulate her ideas and feelings in an informal setting. Those who underestimate their talents experience the fear of feeling not quite good enough. Those who overestimate their talents don't know what they don't know, and therefore can't set out to learn it.

Now that you have identified those leadership skills you want to improve, the final step is to practice, practice, practice. The place to begin is with mundane assignments others often refuse: taking minutes at meetings, serving as chair of the social committee, doing PowerPoint presentations, and introducing speakers. These opportunities give you practice and place you near the center of the action and power. A person who attended one of our leadership seminars described his experience in taking minutes:

> The chair of the committee asked who wanted to take the minutes, heads turned downward and no one volunteered. I said that I would. I discovered that I could write interesting and sometimes humorous notes, and this record was always read at the beginning of each meeting, thus setting the tone for the committee's work. I was part of the action.

The amazing thing about practice is that it leads to self-confidence and enjoyment. And there is a bonus, best expressed by Gary Player: "The harder I practice, the luckier I get" (Brubaker, 1988, p. 8).

The personal and professional rewards in meeting this creative curriculum leadership challenge are many, but perhaps the most satisfying is to participate in something larger than oneself, for it is in using those talents that interest us that we create each other in community.

GUIDELINES FOR KEEPING THE FIRE

The five steps discussed thus far in this chapter are complemented by the following guidelines for keeping the fire. Enjoy your secret aspirations, for they are images that will drive you forward and map your future. A prominent newscaster described the role of secret aspirations he held as a child: "My parents divorced when I was in my early teens and so I was sent to a small town in West Virginia with my father, who was an alcoholic. There was many a night when I would pull my father out of a snowbank near our front door." He added, "I sat at my school desk and thought about how I would get out of this situation and make a better life for myself. A few caring teachers shared my dream and made a difference in my life." The newscaster's dream was at first a general direction, something he creatively brooded about before seeing specific details that would lead to concrete action (Brubaker & Kinard, 1988).

A second guideline is to start wherever you are right now to set new directions. It is a delusion to think that you can jump right to the top and be an accomplished performer. The prominent newscaster's career began with a radio audition in a small town, at which he was asked to read three items: a commercial, a public service announcement, and an obituary. He didn't get the announcer's position, but instead was offered a job sweeping floors and filing records at $7.50 a week. This gave him access to the station's control board and the opportunity to practice radio announcing.

A creative curriculum leader was bothered by anxiety over speech making to the extent that he was losing sleep. He talked to a friend who is a nationally recognized public speaker. The friend said, "The place to start learning to speak better is in any group that will invite you." The anxious speaker took his advice and began speaking at local civic groups and the like. After several years of practice, he is not an outstanding speaker, but he is good enough so that he sleeps better.

The third guideline is that there is no substitute for spontaneity. Pretension is the enemy of authenticity, a key to creative leadership. M. Scott Peck (1993) speaks to the matter of pretension and rigidity: "Most of the evil in this world—the incivility—is committed by people who are absolutely certain that they know what they're doing" (p. 91).

It sounds ironic, but the secret to spontaneity (and enjoying yourself) is not to take any one thing too seriously. To do so is to lose one's sense of humor. An educator said to me, "The best time I ever had was when I was roasted at a banquet when I announced my retirement." He had learned to laugh at life and himself.

Concentrating on the task at hand can be another way of keeping the fire. This takes attention off of you and allows the natural warmth of your personality to come forward. Whether you are talking to a group or an individual, make eye contact and speak from your heart. Warmth and confidence will follow.

One also keeps the fire alive by passing the torch to others. We feel the pride of ownership when we give our creative energies to what we value, but this pride is empty if we don't have others to share what we are creating. Each of us can remember someone who saw in us talents that we didn't recognize in ourselves. We are challenged to pass on this gift to others. The previously mentioned newscaster felt this in his first speech class: "I had an exceptional teacher who reassured me from those first embarrassing moments in giving a speech in class that I could do it."

Another guideline rarely discussed is that there is no substitute for having someone who loves you unconditionally. It is not fashionable, particularly for men, to talk about love as the driving force in their lives. Yet conversations with men in leadership seminars have taught us that the support of significant, caring people in their lives has made all of the difference. Giving our resources to creating bridges rather than walls moves us away from a zero-sum way of seeing others. The more we give to each other, the more we seem to get from each other.

How Will I Know If the Fire Is Alive?

First, the anxiety of actually doing things will subside as the process of doing them unfolds. Second, your resources will be devoted to building, rather than tearing down. You will feel less inclined to criticize others and will enjoy what you're doing more. Third, others' opinions of how you perform will be less important than your own enjoyment of it. Trying to please everybody is an impossible and frustrating goal.

The metaphor of banking the coals in old-fashioned iron stoves to preserve the fire on the most frigid nights is a useful one. When you go to bed at night, concentrate on banking the coals in your mind. Allow the brain, a marvelous instrument, to create new concepts while you sleep. Think of the seemingly mundane acts that you perform each day as a creative curriculum leader as banking the coals for more critical tasks ahead. There are also times when problems seem to overwhelm us. Distance and reflection have a way of creating avenues to their own resolution. Morning often brings a refreshing interpretation to the quandary of the previous day.

Banking the fire for problem resolution is far more profitable than dwelling on a problem, as many of us are prone to do. Time, distance, reflection, and interpretation allow the embers of the fire the space to create new and more distinct images of life's challenges.

CONCLUSION

You will be motivated to further your vocation or calling, and develop your curriculum, by knowing ways to keep the fire. Because of the uniqueness of each person, there is no one set of steps or guidelines that will work for all educators. Rather, it is our challenge to find those ways that work for us as individuals. It is the sharing of what we learn through this process that once again helps us create community.

Case 7: Contradictory Messages About Motivation for Teaching

You have attended one of the best orientation speeches by a superintendent of schools that you have ever heard. Several thousand teachers and administrators applauded the superintendent for his stirring message. The central part of his speech was that the "buzz words" of education, such as "standards-based curriculum," are not the heart of education. The real motivation for teaching, according to the superintendent, is your relationship as a teacher with children in the classroom and school.

You return to your school for the orientation meeting that the principal will conduct. The principal, who is poised and articulate, gives a motivational speech on the new standards-based curriculum plan that she has had exposure to over the summer. Emphasis is on these programs as the solution to problems in the school rather than on the relationship between teachers and students.

After lunch you return to the school to discuss the morning's activities with your leadership team. What will you say? Please choose from the following alternatives:

1. The superintendent is right. Take the message to heart and ignore the principal's speech.

2. The principal's message is the one you live with each day. Take her message to heart, and ignore the superintendent's speech.

3. You know by now that contradictory messages are par for the course. Do what you think is right as a professional person.

Case 7: Rationales for the Alternative Responses

1. The superintendent is obviously right. There are so many buzz words surrounding education that you know by now the programs attached to them come and go. To depend on such buzz words and programs to keep the fire leads to a superficial professional style. Simply to try to implement the superintendent's speech without further reflection, however, fails to consider the culture of your school. Consider a better response.

2. It is certainly true that you have to live with your principal as the primary person who sets the tone for the culture of your school. You also know from experience, however, that your principal will begin each year by trying to implement the most recent buzz words and programs. Simply to try to implement the principal's most recent message is to live a superficial life, adjusting to this externally located authority. Seek a better response.

3. Motivation, or keeping the fire, has to be internally located to really make a difference. The superintendent's message is on target, and the principal is off base. Take this information and point of view to your leadership committee and use it as the basis for discussion. You will have to participate in the principal's most recent pet programs, but recognize that you as a professional are the artist who will make a difference in relating to students and colleagues. This is the best response.

Case 8: Colleague Asks Advice About Dealing With Anxiety and Depression

A colleague and friend at work takes you aside after the school day is over and says the following to you:

I am one of the few school principals who left the principalship to return to teaching. I never told you all of the reasons why I left the principalship, and I haven't told you what has happened to me since I left the principalship. When the principalship got to me, I said, "Why am I responsible for all of these irresponsible people?" What I really meant was that there seemed to be no getting away from the responsibility of the job. I never learned to pace myself. I remember the day that I sat down and typed out my resignation. A great sense of relief came over me.

What I didn't expect is what I am experiencing now. Even though I got a letter from the superintendent of schools saying what a good job I did, and even though I always got high evaluations at the end of each year, *I feel like I failed*. I still can't sleep well at night, and I am starting to develop phobias that seem to overcome me at times. When I was a principal, I suffered from anxiety, but now I really feel depressed. What should I do?

Please choose the best of the following alternatives:

1. Listen carefully and support your friend in any way, short of giving specific advice.

2. Listen to your friend carefully, give support, and recommend talking to the principal.

3. Listen to your friend carefully, give support, and recommend talking to his or her family physician.

4. Listen to your friend carefully, give support, recommend talking to his or her family physician, but add that he or she may wish to also talk to a psychologist, counselor, or psychiatrist if the family physician isn't helpful.

Case 8: Rationales for the Alternative Responses

1. By listening to your friend carefully you will be giving support, but you won't hazard possible difficulties of giving advice. In a matter like this, only experts can give advice, and you aren't an expert. The problem with this response is that your friend is asking for advice and appears to be suffering a good deal. By not meeting his or her request, you may communicate a lack of support. Consider other alternatives for a better response.

2. By listening to your friend and giving advice you will demonstrate your concern and care. Your recommendation to talk to his or her principal may or may not be a good idea, depending on the principal. If the principal is a competent and caring person, it will be helpful to have the designated leader's support at work. If the principal is insensitive—or worse yet, the kind of leader who could hold this over your friend's head, it would be a serious mistake to talk to the principal at this point, perhaps at any point. The possible difficulties with this response should probably prompt you to look at other alternatives.

3. Listening and caring are important first steps. Your friend's description of his or her pain and request for advice should tell you that more serious measures are called for. The family physician should know something about situations like this and is also bound by professional code to discretion. The family physician also has a medical network in place and can recommend a psychiatrist or psychologist if necessary. The drawback with this option is that the family physician may or may not be expert enough in such matters to help your friend. Some are, and some aren't. Therefore, consider a better response.

4. Listening to your friend and caring is an important first step. This honest sharing of information regarding anxiety and depression, plus your friend's request for advice, indicates that he or she is serious about the pain and difficulties. Therefore, advise your friend to seek professional help in the event that the family physician doesn't give advice that eases the pain. Make it clear that you will support him or her by caring and being a good listener at any time during counseling. This is probably the best response, although Alternative 3 is also a good response.

PART III

Curriculum Development Can Make a Difference

It is simply a truism that educators exist within organizations, and one's attitudes are part of larger mind-sets (paradigms) toward such organizations. Occasionally, there is a radical change in an educator's mind-set, something that may be called *a paradigm shift*. Gerald Austin, former superintendent of schools and a National Football League head referee, describes a paradigm shift that occurred after reading *Creative Survival in Educational Bureaucracies* (Brubaker & Nelson, 1974). As he explained it, "I used to think I was severely constricted by organizations. Then I realized that *once you know what the rules are, everything else is open to you*" (Austin, 1993).

Austin implies that there are three dimensions to leadership: (a) *what is,* including what the rules are; (b) *what should be,* one's personal and organizational vision; and (c) *what can be,* the art of the possible or the political. These three aspects of decision making lead us to the power of knowing how to critique. That is, the decision maker reviews what is going on, adopts a point of view in relation to what is observed, and then supports this point of view in light of what is possible. A former superintendent of schools in a large metropolitan school system, Edward Lakey, describes this process:

> I had only been on the job for three months when asked to appear on a half-hour television news program. While on the way to the station, the deputy superintendent asked me what I planned to say. I replied, "It all boils down to this. This system has had a history of nepotism—hiring people because they are someone's relatives or friends. This practice has not been in the best interest of children and the system as a whole. Under my administration we're going to hire the best-qualified person for the job. Excellent schools depend on hiring excellent staff and I'm going to use all of the resources I have to build an excellent school system."

As a superintendent of schools, Edward Lakey didn't always get his way on this matter with the school board, but his realistic critique of the situation he inherited was a kind of map for daily decision making. His personal and organizational vision served as a beacon of light that guided him through troubled waters. In short, he had integrity, a basic element of character (Covey, 1989). He had defined and empowered himself (Steinem, 1992). His personal curriculum development was the substructure for creative leadership in the school system. He demonstrated that critique, as with all evaluation, is *personal*.

Chapter 6, "Creative Curriculum Leadership in Practice," discusses what happens when the educator interested in developing his or her own curriculum applies such knowledge to learning settings. This chapter weds the inner curriculum and the outer curriculum: what each person experiences as learning settings are cooperatively created and the course of study. Chapter 7, "Civility in Leadership: The Ultimate Difference," describes what happens in learning settings when educators give attention to the character issue. It is argued that such attention makes all the difference in the kinds of relationships professional educators and others experience.

Chapter 8, "Creating Learning Communities," describes how the creative curriculum leader can help educators build their *social capital* in the interest of helping others and themselves as lifelong learners. This is a special challenge in a society where a sense of community has been eroded. Chapter 9, "Teacher Leaders," was written to help the reader rethink teachers' work. Teacher leaders within learning communities are in a position to help their colleagues who are teachers and administrators; this help is valuable both in its own right and also as preparatory experience in the event that they want to enter school and school system administration.

6

Creative Curriculum Leadership in Practice

In college I used my intellectual skills to get good grades by knowing the right answers. But at work, I found out that knowing the right answer was only 10 percent of the battle. Working with people was the other 90 percent. And we hadn't learned that at school.

—McCall, Lombardo, and
Morrison (1988, p. 22)

This quote is from a college graduate who described the shift from the culture of higher education to the culture of the work world. For our purposes, the graduate makes the point that human endeavor, rather than scientific pursuit, is at the center of creative curriculum leadership. I have argued in this book that the creative curriculum leader uses his or her talents to help others identify and use their talents. This role for the curriculum leader is quite different from the role commonly prescribed; namely, the leader gets others to do what he or she wants them to do, regardless of whether they want to do it. The commonly prescribed role has a scientific management ring to it, the ring of manipulation and top-down power arrangements.

We will see in this chapter that the creative curriculum leader is challenged to establish lateral relationships with others, so that they are empowered to develop their own new directions for themselves within the organizational structure of schools and school systems.

We begin our discussion of creative curriculum leadership by describing and discussing four kinds of covenants or relationships with persons that vary with respect to *intensity* and *duration* (Brubaker, 1982b). We enter into covenants with other persons to assure predictability in our relationships. Entering into an agreement to play tennis with another person is a useful metaphor. Players agree to accept certain rules of the game so that one's expertise, rather than one's ability to cheat, is at stake: The boundaries of the court are lined, a ball that falls on a line is playable, the player serving has two serves per point, and so forth. In short, one's flexibility or choice of options is diminished in the interest of predictability, but this predictability in turn assures players of a kind of freedom because less time and emotional effort are needed than would be the case if chaos prevailed.

A similar situation exists for the curriculum leader. Dependable relationships help the curriculum leader distinguish between the possible and the impossible. The head of a curriculum committee needs to know which members of the committee will probably attend meetings, and also needs to assess their abilities and commitments, to know what they can be expected to do if certain tasks are to be completed. Committee members need similar information about the curriculum leader.

COVENANT 1: LITTLE INTENSITY AND BRIEF DURATION

Our technologically advanced society encourages many covenants that are pleasant but taken lightly. They also don't last very long. The seasoned airplane passenger experiences this kind of covenant. Flight attendants and others are pleasant and, in fact, frequently act as if they are creating another home setting for the customer. If you recognized a flight attendant in a department store later in the day, you probably wouldn't go out of your way to say hello in spite of congenial rhetoric earlier in the day.

As a curriculum leader you may be asked to give a brief speech that introduces the audience to the curriculum-planning process. Or you may be asked to either head or be a member of an ad hoc curriculum group that meets briefly, simply to justify a decision an administrator has already made. Both of these situations are examples of covenants of little intensity and brief duration.

COVENANT 2: HIGH INTENSITY AND BRIEF DURATION

If you are an infrequent airplane passenger who is anxious about flying, the thirty-minute flight is probably intense, in spite of its brief duration. I encountered such a person on a flight from Williamsport, Pennsylvania, to Philadelphia. He drank his own two alcoholic beverages as well as two his wife had ordered before slowly disembarking from the airplane.

As a curriculum leader, you may be asked to be a member of an accreditation team that makes an on-site visit to a host organization for a few days. Team members immerse themselves in the evaluation process literally night and day. The importance of the task draws team members into a close working relationship, at the end of which a report is written and members go their separate ways. Another example is a curriculum retreat, where persons work closely together in a relatively isolated setting for a brief period of time. There is often an adjustment period when participants return to their home settings and find that such settings have a life of their own that is quite different from the retreat setting.

COVENANT 3: NOT INTENSE BUT LONG TERM

A curriculum leader may be assigned to a committee that has a ritualistic function, which must be carried out infrequently for the year or for several years. The commencement committee in a particularly tradition-oriented setting serves as an example. Some committees that give scholarships to students are also of this nature. They meet several times during the year to make decisions about who gets what scholarships, but their deliberations are largely perfunctory, as are the deliberations of the commencement committee that meets several times a year and simply affirms traditionally made decisions.

COVENANT 4: INTENSE AND LONG TERM

The final kind of covenant is the rarest. You, the curriculum leader, may be assigned to a long-range planning committee that is expected to meet for three years. During this time, you meet almost weekly and make a number of difficult decisions that will affect persons in the organization. For example, you may recommend the elimination of some programs and the diminution of others—decisions that affect the lives of organization members as well as their families and friends.

You are probably at the place where you wonder how the covenant framework is useful to you as a creative curriculum leader. To help others identify and use their talents, the creative curriculum leader is aware of the opportunities each kind of covenant offers. For example, Covenant 1, little intensity and brief duration, gives people with ritualistic talents a chance to use them. Some people are truly gifted in ceremonial roles. They are able to stand up, often on a moment's notice, and represent your school or school system well. Covenant 2, high intensity and brief duration, affords some people a chance to operate under pressure for a brief time, after which they can move on to the next challenge. Unlike the tortoise, the hare runs in spurts. So, too, do some curriculum leaders show their excellence in brief, pressure-packed situations. People with these talents usually do best in ad hoc task-oriented situations, where reports are due. Covenant 3, low intensity but long term, also gives people with ritualistic talents the opportunity to stand up, speak eloquently, and then move back. Faculty meetings are sometimes led by people with these talents. Some educators handle details well when there is little pressure. They do well with Covenant 3 activities. Covenant 4, intense and long term, demands curriculum leaders who will stay the course and have good follow-through. The intense nature of the long-term commitment demands leaders who are not fickle or rigid and who handle pressure well. Primarily, this kind of covenant calls for a person with well-honed people skills (Brubaker & Simon, 1993).

It should be clear that the curriculum leader's attitude toward a particular person or committee dictates the kind of covenant that is formed. For example, if a school principal strongly believes in shared decision making, the leadership team or committee will probably enter into a highly intense and long-term covenant with the principal and with one another. If the principal views shared decision making as a ritualistic requirement of the superintendent, the leadership team will enter into a low-intensity but long-term covenant with the principal and one another.

It is also the case that a formally designated committee, such as the shared decision-making leadership team or committee will sometimes simply fail to deliver over the course of a fairly long period of time, after which the principal will turn to another committee to do the job. For example, in one school where I was a consultant, the shared decision-making committee turned into a "gripe group" because half of its members refused to think positively. They were experiencing difficult home situations that spilled over into their school lives. The principal worked with the team diligently, trying to help overcome the negativism, but her intervention didn't work. The principal, therefore, turned to the social committee as her core group or governance group, and the school climate improved considerably. This simply demonstrates that there is no one generalization that holds for all people in all situations. The principal and other curriculum leaders must have contingency plans and use their artistry.

The covenant framework may also be useful to the curriculum leader as an evaluation device. The creative curriculum leader can diagnose present relationships in a setting, some of which involve him or her, and others that involve other persons. The framework is also helpful in evaluating relationships that emerge during involvement in the curriculum development process. The curriculum leader can see how many and what kinds of relationships have formed in his or her own and others' professional lives. The framework can also serve the creative curriculum leader in planning for relationships he or she would like to see exist.

The previous discussion demonstrates that the creative curriculum leader knows that reaching important goals is not a solitary activity. It is therefore necessary to create a core group, whose members' commitment to each other is both intense and long lasting (Covenant 4). Core group members are in effect a leadership team who together afford emotional support and serve as a sounding board for sharpening ideas. In short, core group members are engaged in praxis, or reflective action, in the community.

In conclusion, the creative curriculum leader is aware of the value of all four kinds of covenants and initiates or participates in each to the best of his or her ability. It is a basic tenet of contingency theory that one's best choice of alternatives depends on the specific variables in a given situation (Peck, 1993).

Six Ways of Relating to Others

Stephen Covey, author of the excellent book, *The 7 Habits of Highly Effective People* (1989) identifies six paradigms or mindsets of human interaction. The creative curriculum leader can use this framework to identify and assess his or her leadership patterns as well as the patterns of others. Before identifying and describing the six ways of interacting with others, I would like to introduce a simulation game that will place you in the role of decision maker within the six-part framework. This game, swimming the Amazon, is one I use in leadership seminars. It is based on an annual event in my swimming group.

Imagine for a moment that you are a respectable but not outstanding swimmer, who swims a mile five times a week in an after-school adult swimming group. There are approximately ten other swimmers in your group. When you arrive at the pool on a Monday evening in January, the head lifeguard hands out a photocopied sheet with the headline, "Welcome to the Amazon River Swim." The sheet explains that if you are interested in joining this swim, you should sign a sheet on the bulletin board at the end of the pool. Then, it is noted, you will be assigned a colored stick pin with your initials written on masking tape at the top of the pin. Your challenge is to swim the Amazon River, twenty-five miles in the pool, over a six-week period. It is each participant's job as an honor swimmer to move his or her pin to the next mile mark on the bulletin board's drawing of the Amazon River. The sheet concludes by saying that you will receive a free T-shirt when your pin reaches the end (mouth) of the Amazon River.

You decide to accept the challenge and sign your name on the entrance sheet. The next day your pin is at the bottom of the Amazon River, and at the end of each swim you move your pin forward, toward the end of the river at the top of the bulletin board. You don't pay much attention to other pins on the board until, lo and behold, you see that your pin has reached the top of the bulletin board before all other pins reach this place.

What will you do with your pin? Why? If you are reading this in a solitary setting, please write your answers to these questions. If you are in a group setting, share your answers with the group.

Let us now identify and describe six ways of interacting with others, after which you will be asked to locate your response, to where you will place your pin, in one of the categories.

Win–Win leaves all parties in the interaction with a good feeling about the decision and a common commitment to this decision and concrete next steps. The general mind-set is one of cooperation rather than competition. Covey (1989) argues that "most situations, in fact, are part of an interdependent reality, and then Win–Win is really the only viable alternative" (p. 211).

Win–Lose places you in a position where you always compare your results to those of others. "No recognition is given to intrinsic value; everyone is extrinsically defined" (Covey, 1989, p. 208). Life is viewed as an arena where competition is both inevitable and desirable. Athletic contests are the most prominent metaphor for the Win–Lose paradigm, for there is clearly a winner and a loser. Covey concludes: "Certainly there is a place for Win–Lose thinking in truly competitive and low-trust situations. But most of life is not a competition" (pp. 208–209).

Lose–Win people are frequently happy only when they are pleasing and receiving the approbation of others. To compensate for their own lack of confidence, they live through the victories of others. But the problem, according to Covey (1989) is that Lose–Win people bury a lot of feelings. He adds, "And unexpressed feelings never die: they're buried alive and come forth later in uglier ways" (p. 209).

Lose–Lose people are usually rigid, stubborn, and ego-invested (Covey, 1989). "Miscry loves company" people are also often Lose–Lose people, for they only find direction in joining losing causes with like-minded people.

Win people don't necessarily want someone else to lose. That's irrelevant; what matters is that they get what they want (Covey, 1989, p. 210). As one leader said, "My philosophy is to get out front and then let others see what I've accomplished."

Win–Win or *No Deal* people agree to disagree agreeably (Covey, 1989). They simply don't want to make a deal. In short, they refuse to play the competitive game. They sometimes communicate the feeling that "I'm above the game" by refusing to play it, or they simply go away so as to not get in the fray.

Please turn to the chart that follows and place your answers to the Amazon River Swim Game in the box that best defines your response. If you are in a group setting, place the names of others in your group in respective boxes after discussing in the group where such responses fall.

After you have participated in the first part of this exercise, imagine that you have just been named the principal of a school of your choice, or superintendent of a school system of your choice. Most new leaders are allowed to hire one trusted person from their old setting as a high-level assistant in the new setting. *Who in your group setting will you hire and why?* (Their responses to the Amazon River Swim Game must be used as the basis for your decision.)

You may be interested in some other participants' responses to the Amazon River Swim Game:

Win–Win people often say, "I would leave my pin at the mouth of the Amazon and wait for others. I may even slow myself down so that we can cross the line together. I believe in team victories."

Win–Lose participants say things such as, "I would start over again with my pin and see how many others I could lap.

Or else I would place my pin at the top left side of the bulletin board, with the number one to the left of my name, which I would spell out in large letters."

Lose–Win people often make comments such as, "My satisfaction would come in seeing others cross the finish line. I would especially like to see some of the slower swimmers do well. Let someone else get eaten by the alligators. Others would be inspired and shocked to see me win."

Lose–Lose game players make comments like, "It is impossible to win" and "There are nothing but losers in this game."

Win swimmers say that their finishing first would be recognized and appreciated by themselves as winners. "I would just leave my pin at the top of the board," a Win participant said. She added, "I would get no satisfaction in seeing that others didn't finish first. That would be mean."

Win–Win or *No Deal* people simply refuse to say what they will do with their pins if all who play can't be winners. The game isn't worth playing if there have to be winners and losers.

There tend to be two general patterns in choosing an assistant in the new setting. The newly chosen principal or superintendent either chooses someone who has the same orientation to interacting with others, or someone who has a very different style that will complement the organizational head's style.

WIN–WIN	WIN–LOSE	LOSE–WIN
LOSE–LOSE	WIN	WIN–WIN or NO DEAL

Amazon River Swim Game

Now that you have participated in the Amazon River Swim Game and have placed responses in the six-part interaction framework, what guidelines can you identify for relating competition and cooperation to each other?

The following guidelines have been generated by leadership seminar participants:

1. Know who you are in relation to competition and cooperation.

2. Be all that you can be. You have to be able to compete and be a team player. Don't feel guilty if you win. (You don't need to pay interest on a debt you don't owe.)

3. Be yourself. Don't pretend to be someone you aren't. Enjoy who you are and be able to laugh at some of the funny things that happen because of who you are.

4. Be patient. The race went to the tortoise, not the hare.

A Sense of Vision

The creative curriculum leader is expected to give attention to both personal and organizational vision. As Lloyd DuVall (1989) said,

If you don't care where you are going, any trip will do! But, adults and children interested in a school are not content to have leaders who are simply happy wanderers. Members within the school culture want to assign meaning to their activities, and it is this sense of direction or vision that can, if developed and articulated well, provide such meaning.

Father Theodore Martin Hesburgh, president of the University of Notre Dame from 1952 to 1987, said it best: "The very essence of leadership is you have to have a vision. You can't blow an uncertain trumpet" (Austin & Brubaker, 1988, p. 104). When there is a shared vision, all are proud to be part of the organization. This serves as an essential element in self-management. The creative leader helps to create the conditions whereby others become their own leaders. They are motivated to give their best because they are on a team that is committed to important values. The value of such teamwork was related to the author by a teacher who headed the school's advisory council: "If there is no teamwork, everybody wastes resources in covering their backsides; when there is teamwork, trust replaces suspicion, people are willing to make themselves vulnerable and clear lines of communication exist."

Vision can sometimes help people in dramatic difficulty. Stephen Callahan spent seventy-six lonely days at sea after his sailboat capsized. How did he make it through his despair? "Dreams, ideas, and plans not only are an escape, they gave me purpose, a reason to hang on" (Callahan, 1986, p. 63). Creative curriculum leaders also find a sense of vision helpful to them when times are tough—for example, when there are interpersonal difficulties with a principal or superintendent of schools. But vision is equally important to us as we do the simple, mundane things each day. Actor Richard Dreyfuss talks about the importance of his vision of growing up and maturing: "It's thrilling. I enjoy even doing little things that I disdained before, like color-coordinating what I'm wearing, not looking like a jerk. It's the simple pleasure of behaving like a normal human being" (Dreyfuss, 1986). So, too, is this true for the creative curriculum leader involved in the details of each day at work.

It is a reality of our age that there is a scarcity of resources. The curriculum leader is expected to allocate such resources wisely. Quite simply this means that priorities must be set. The curriculum leader continually asks himself or herself, "What do I value more than something else?" It is helpful to identify one's own values in a general or abstract way, but one quickly discovers that it is the specific content of one's values, and the contingency of variables, that are the critical matter with respect to priority setting.

In one elementary school, for example, teachers and students in a wing of the school were continually cold because of a faulty heating system. The leadership team committee, strongly supported by the rhetoric of the principal, pressured the principal to do something about this matter. The principal worked through channels, but in the meantime that wing of the building remained cold. The leadership team committee, taking the principal and the superintendent of schools at their word on the value of shared decision making, wrote a memorandum to the board of education, giving specifics about the heating problem. The superintendent of schools was irate, but the principal walked his talk and supported the shared decision-making committee and the faculty they represented.

A second example involves a proactive teacher, Judy, who wishes to initiate a curriculum-planning project in a school system whose superintendent is unwilling to commit many resources to any project that leaves him off the steering committee. Judy faces a dilemma: A basic tenet of the project is local control with power primarily in the hands of team leaders in each school, but the superintendent feels threatened by this tenet unless his presence on the steering committee is a reality. Judy will need to set priorities within the context of these realities to achieve as many of the goals and objectives as possible.

If Judy decides to invite the superintendent to be a member of the steering committee, she will probably receive more resources for her project, which will help persons at the local level feel more relaxed about what can be done. (They won't have to worry about phone bills, supplies, secretarial support, and the like.) At the same time, Judy will risk having the superintendent exert his positional authority on the project, which will be a threat to local control.

Let us imagine that Judy decides not to invite the superintendent to be a member of the steering committee, so resources for the project are severely limited. The result may well be a kind of bureaucratic monitoring of the use of limited resources, with persons at the local level tense about what can be done. (Approval forms will have to be filled out for the use of the telephone, the acquisition of materials, travel money, and the like, with little hope of receiving many of these resources.)

In the first instance, where the superintendent is formally involved and resources are plentiful, general goals will be emphasized, with trust given to persons expected to reach these more general curriculum-planning ends. In the second instance, where resources are scarce, greater emphasis will probably be given to behavioral objectives because administrators will probably be nervous about not going over the budget. A lack of trust will therefore be communicated to project members. The monitoring of the budget will create the kind of bureaucratic central control that Judy originally intended to avoid.

In effect, Judy's decision to include or not include the superintendent can lead to a similar result. She must decide which decision will be least likely to threaten her original goal of giving local control to project members. In short, she will set priorities in accordance with her vision for the project.

THE HISTORY OF THE SETTING

Setting is a term or concept that may be useful to the creative curriculum leader. A setting is "any instance when two or more people come together in new and sustained relationships to achieve common goals" (Sarason, 1972, p. ix). Examples of settings are a classroom in the fall, a new state organization for principals, and the formation of a leadership team in a school. When a new setting is created, it of necessity encounters the history of a previous setting.

Creative curriculum leaders avoid giving attention to the history of the setting at their own peril. Yet curriculum leaders are tempted to act as if life began with the first day they entered the setting or began creating the setting. Such a position flatters the leader's ego and makes no demands on him or her to study systematically what came before the beginning influences (Sarason, 1972). A dramatic representation of this took place at our home a few years ago. A guest arrived at the front door two hours after a party began and said, "Oh, the party has just begun, huh?" I responded, "No, it looks that way to you since you just got here." (Have you ever had this feeling about the behavior of a new principal or superintendent of schools?)

The challenge to the creative curriculum leader interested in creating a setting is to relate to the setting's zeitgeist, or what's in the air; what is in the air derives from the existing social structure (Sarason, 1972, p. 25). More specifically, the curriculum leader needs to understand *ways of thinking* (assumptions and conceptions) different from his or her own ways of thinking (Sarason, 1972). Why is this? It is simply because "the new setting proposed by the curriculum leader confronts a preexisting complicated structure of relationships, parts of which work against and parts that work for the creation of a new setting"(Sarason, 1972, p. 42).

The following questions may be helpful to the curriculum leader in relating to the history of the setting (Sarason, 1972).

Is the need for a new setting clearly recognized by a substantial element of the old setting? If the answer to this question is yes, the curriculum leader is more likely to be invited to introduce changes in the old setting. If the answer is no, the curriculum leader may well be considered a troublemaker who wants to disrupt routines that have provided comfort and security to those in the old setting.

Was the need for a new setting openly voiced and therefore initiated by those within the old setting? In the previous question, the key word was *recognized*, but in the present question the key words are *openly voiced* and *initiated*. If the members of the old setting reached the point where they openly voiced their need for a new setting, they probably ran some risk in doing so. If they actually initiated a new setting while being part of the old setting, they clearly bought into the change process. (In many settings, unhappy persons are passively aggressive: They don't help those who wish to perpetuate the old setting; neither do they openly challenge such persons, but rather they undercut their efforts.) The curriculum leader needs to identify key persons who have given resources to openly voicing the need for a new setting and taking action to initiate the construction of a new setting.

Our experience is that the chances of success in creating a new setting are greatly enhanced if the need for a new setting is clearly recognized and voiced by key leaders in the old setting, and if such persons initiate action on behalf of the creation of a new setting. Persons in settings frequently say that they see no need for changes. Furthermore, they add, they are tired of outsiders coming in and trying to introduce things without asking whether people in the setting want such changes.

Do those who initiated the drive toward the creation of a new setting recognize the importance of understanding the history of the setting? If not, they run the risk of counterforces that they never anticipated. A department chairperson in a high school wanted to create a new setting involving her seven-member staff. Carried away with her enthusiasm for the new setting, she failed to discover that most staff members were secure in their bureaucratic relationship with the previous chairperson. The less authoritarian, shared decision-making plan she wanted to initiate was considered a threat, so the new setting had little chance for survival.

Are those interested in creating a new setting clear as to their goals and objectives as well as the predominant goals and objectives held by members of the old setting? Sometimes a person's enthusiasm for the new setting prompts him or her to give attention to activities, with goals and objectives neglected. Total attention to activities can lead to an interesting carnival atmosphere, in which events have no common threads or directions. In short, there is no meaning for the curriculum program or project. Curriculum planners sometimes encounter such a situation, whereby subgroups occupy themselves with activities, but the total group seems to lack rationale for its existence.

Do members of the old setting recognize that persons generally have unlimited desires, but the setting has limited resources? The curriculum leader will sometimes find that members of the old setting who want changes believe that simply wanting them will bring them about. Such persons haven't squarely faced the fact that resources are always limited, and enthusiasm for change isn't enough in itself. (How difficult is it for a honeymoon couple to sit down before the honeymoon and discuss what they might not be able to do because of limited resources?)

Is the rhetoric of those in the old setting consistent with the degree of commitment they exhibit in their actions? The curriculum leader will sometimes encounter persons in the old setting whose rhetoric outdistances their commitment to action. A physically active teacher polled faculty members throughout the school to find out if they were interested in becoming corporate members of a nearby athletic club. Because only fifteen responses were needed to buy such a membership, the teacher was happily surprised by the thirty potential members who signed forms. A month later, when dues were supposed to be sent to the athletic club, only five of the thirty had sent in their membership fees. The initial reaction of the teacher who initiated action was one of bitterness. "Never again," he moaned.

What kinds of covenants have members of the old setting formed, and what kinds do they say they would like to have in the future? Using the covenant formation framework in an earlier part of this chapter, the curriculum leader can construct a profile of the old setting by noting the kinds of covenants already formed. An early diagnosis of possible future relationships can also be made as the curriculum leader converses with members of the old setting about relationships they would like to have in the future.

Do leaders who are interested in creating a new setting see their role as a matter of chance, or as part of the natural history of events? The emergence of leadership at a particular time in a setting's history is part of the natural evolution of that setting, and yet many leaders fail to see this. Rather, they consider it a matter of chance. The curriculum leader needs to identify and analyze those forces that brought him or her to power at this time in the history of the setting.

Do leaders who wish to create a new setting act as if all members of the old setting want to be invited to play some role in the creation of the new setting? The curriculum leader interested in creating a new setting may be enticed to think that all members of the old setting don't want to be (or shouldn't be) invited to join in creating the new setting, but in fact all are flattered by the invitation, regardless of whether they make this known publicly. The challenge to the curriculum leader is to find appropriate and sometimes subtle ways to involve all members in creating the new setting. In this way, they assume ownership for the creation of the new setting. Meeting this challenge is consistent with the definition of creative leadership: using your talents to help others identify and use their talents.

Do members of the old setting who plan to give leadership to the new setting understand the setting's concept, or do they view changes in narrower terms—such as a series of discrete decisions and actions? It is important that all who will give leadership in creating a new setting share a common view of the context or framework in which change will take place. The setting's concept provides leaders with such a framework. The curriculum leader will probably encounter many members of the old setting who see change as a series of discrete and often unrelated events.

Do members of the old setting who plan to give leadership to the creation of the new setting think in extreme terms, or do they make finer distinctions? It is easy for persons involved in creating something new to think in terms of the good people (those who want to create a new setting) and the bad people (those who oppose the creation of a new setting). To be an effective curriculum leader, one must make finer distinctions that will invite people with many shades of opinions, especially the dissident voice, into the creation process.

In conclusion, the curriculum leader involved in the creation process of a setting is creatively challenged to consider past events, trends, and leadership patterns formed before his or her entrance into the setting. This challenge to the artistry of the creative curriculum leader is what brings life to those who are willing to meet it.

THE CULTURE OF THE SETTING

The history of the setting may be defined as the way we *did* things around here. The culture of the setting is the way we *do* things around here. The basic values of a setting are expressed in its way of life or culture. The creative curriculum leader must consider the culture of a setting, for a culture's imperatives or commands will surely influence what is possible to achieve. A few examples of cultural imperatives follow:

1. All buildings have heavy screens to protect windows from vandalism.

2. Doors to bathrooms are locked between classes to curtail vandalism and physical assaults.

3. All buildings have traditional architecture (for example, ninety-degree corners).

4. Adults stand up much of the day, whereas students in most classes sit behind desks that are smaller than those used by adults.

5. Adults ask most of the questions, and students are expected to provide most of the answers.

This brief list of five existing regularities in a particular school setting points out the distance required to identify cultural imperatives. Seymour Sarason (1971), professor emeritus of psychology at Yale University, urges us to imagine that we are from outer space, with our space platform directly above the institution being studied.

Three concepts are useful to us as we distance ourselves from the culture of a setting to better understand it: symbols, rituals, and myths.

Symbols are concrete expressions of more abstract ideas. A symbol quickly conveys a whole set of emotions. The lectern, for example, symbolizes the positional authority of the teacher. A physical education teacher's warm-up outfit symbolizes an informal leadership style, but the whistle around the physical education teacher's neck symbolizes positional authority of a more formal nature. Common language expressions in a setting also tell us about the culture of the setting. The language used by school psychologists, for example, is quite different from the language used by classroom teachers.

Rituals emerge from human interactions to provide persons with the emotional security associated with predictable behavior. Attendance taking, flag ceremonies, and furniture arrangements serve as examples of rituals in settings. It is inevitable that rituals will emerge in a setting. The curriculum leader can evaluate a setting, using rituals as an indicator of regularities in the setting's culture. The curriculum leader is in the position of introducing new rituals in a setting. For example, a new high school principal decided to hold monthly faculty meetings in classroom areas of each department. Each department introduced the faculty meeting with a brief description of its activities.

Myths are stories persons in a setting create to explain the unexplainable. These myths help the person manipulate tensions about interpersonal relationships. They contain elements of reality and unreality, as demonstrated by the commonly held myth that the boss controls everyone in the setting. If we study the setting carefully, we find that there are many and diverse ways, some ingenious, for getting bosses to do what others want them to do. For example, in one school system where the superintendent prided himself on curriculum leadership, as symbolized by his attendance at curriculum conferences, central office leaders and others used their informal sources of power to influence what conferences the superintendent attended. They prided themselves on their use of such influence.

Finally, the "know thyself" theme of this book, a theme originated in the immortal words of Socrates, is directly related to symbols, rituals, and myths. They are models or constructs we use to create ourselves (May, 1975). Symbols and myths are embodied in ritual. It is useful to each of us not only to know this as a personal life script is acted out, but it is also invaluable to observe and make sense out of the lives of others as they do likewise. The creative curriculum leader's actions set the tone for the culture of the organization she leads. Whether she likes it or not, according to M. Scott Peck (1993), this leader's "personality will become a template for the school, the department, the hospital, the corporation, or the entire business she manages" (p. 258). Once again, for those you lead, you will be the curriculum.

SOURCES OF POWER

In using our talents to help others identify and use their talents, we draw on several sources of power. In discussing these sources of power, we will see how our society's view of them has changed.

Positional authority is power by virtue of one's position in the organization. It is commonly associated with bureaucratic forms of organization, for those with more positional authority give commands to their subordinates who have less. Regardless of the respect, or lack of it, accorded the person with positional authority, the bureaucratic subordinate is expected to obey such commands. Traditionally, it has been drawn on heavily, but observers in the area of leadership education argue that drawing on positional authority is much like using a battery: The more you use it, the less there is to use in the future. They therefore recommend that positional authority should be suspended by the leader whenever possible.

Expertise is a source of power attributed to persons because of their recognized ability to do something well. A curriculum leader in a school may, for example, be recognized as a well-organized person who has demonstrated expertise in writing reports. She is therefore asked to head the accreditation planning team for the school. The ability to organize and articulate ideas is an important kind of expertise essential to the curriculum leadership process.

Succor is an informal kind of power that leaves others with the feeling that they are supported emotionally. It is commonly associated with counseling and coaching. "You can do it" is the message transmitted. Curriculum leaders often reach the place in the curriculum-planning process where they are ready to give up because of a lack of interest on the part of committee members or opposition from a person or group. It is precisely at this point that succor can give momentum to tasks that must be completed. The morale of the group depends on this kind of support.

Charisma is a sort of magnetic charm often equated with sex appeal. Nonverbal messages, such as smiles and nods of approval, are the vehicles of communication used by the charismatic leader. Style of dress and the leader's bearing give added charisma.

The creative curriculum leader integrates the sources of power in a manner appropriate for a particular situation. This integration is based on a realistic assessment of the leader's talents, as well as the talents of fellow team members.

Societal changes in the way we view the sources of power were brought home to me by the story of a forty-year-old teacher, whose mother still lives in the mountains of North Carolina:

Our family doctor in the mountains told my mother that she must immediately prepare herself psychologically and physically for surgery in order to amputate a leg ravaged by diabetes. The general practitioner added that her other leg would also have to be amputated in due time. Our family had always trusted the professional judgment of this physician because of his position of authority. My mother prepared herself for surgery. It just didn't seem right to me, however, and so I talked her into going with me to Winston-Salem, North Carolina, a two-hour drive from our home that we almost never made when we were children. A specialist at Wake Forest's Bowman Gray School of Medicine said that amputation was not necessary, given newly found ways of treating diabetes. My mother has been walking around well for fifteen years on legs our family doctor was preparing to remove.

The story graphically depicts the tremendous changes our society has undergone in relation to the role of positional authority. Such changes challenge the creative curriculum leader to a new kind of artistry in leading others and knowing more about self.

THE AESTHETICS OF CREATING A SETTING

Throughout our discussion of the creative curriculum leader's challenge in creating new settings, references have been made to the artistry of creative curriculum leadership. One sometimes gets the feeling that using one's talents to help others identify and use their talents is much like being a leader of a symphony orchestra. The conductor is not an expert on each instrument, but must use artistry to bring out such expertise in orchestra members.

The title of this section of the chapter, "The Aesthetics of Creating a Setting," intimates a process or movement orientation, rather than a product orientation. A more product-oriented title might have been "The Aesthetics of a Created Setting."

A product, such as a curriculum report or a PowerPoint presentation of an experimental project, is a tangible or concrete expression of a process. Its concreteness makes it a powerful political symbol of progress. Administrators can show off this product as an example of tax money wisely spent or leadership effectively exerted. (Remember, as one wag said, you can accomplish anything if you let the boss get the credit.)

A product is summative of a completed end or result that can be evaluated. Process, on the other hand, is formative. It is not what has been done, but instead what is unfolding or becoming. Those who argue that the purpose of education is to produce people who produce things are uncomfortable with the idea that the purpose of education is to help persons who are in the process of becoming what they can be in relating to self, others, and the environment. Philosopher Martin Buber (1970) refers to this as the difference between the I–It relationship and the I–Thou relationship. Although persons' relationships with things are important, they are (should be) less important than persons' relationships with others and oneself (Buber, 1970). Products, the fruit of our labor, should not be denigrated, for they are benchmarks that tell us something of our progress, and their relative permanence lends itself to evaluation, pride, and a sense of efficacy.

Process gives us a sense of the fluidity of life's forces. These forces are always changing and challenging us to change. They encourage us to have a growing edge, which in turn serves as an incentive for further growth and development. The growing edge may be referred to as reconceptualization, for in the process of creating a setting, we learn to see the familiar in unfamiliar ways and the unfamiliar in familiar ways. On the one hand, the curriculum leader involved in the aesthetic process of creating a setting moves into the actor role, and it is in this role that he or she views members of the setting and the environment in different ways. (It is as if someone who has repeatedly sat in the back of an auditorium suddenly decides to sit in the front row.) At the same time, the curriculum leader involved in the aesthetic process of creating a setting perceives familiar happenings, such as traditional arrangements of furniture in meetings, in different ways; the leader now has the power to change such arrangements and set the stage for important committee decisions. The main benefit of being a proactive leader is that you can make things happen.

A second dimension of the aesthetics of creating a setting, one that complements emphasis on process, is that of giving attention to oneself. Those who only give attention to helping others learn not to relate to their own feelings of doubt, joy, pain, and ecstasy. Rather, such persons project their own values and beliefs on others, without really understanding either their own feelings or those of the people being helped.

Seymour Sarason, who has written so much and so well about the creation of settings, relates that he and his colleagues chose to create meaning and pleasure for themselves as they created the Yale Psycho-Educational Clinic: "We were going to judge ourselves only secondarily by how helpful we were to others. Conceivably we would not be very helpful, and conceivably we might even be harmful and yet be successful in terms of personal learning and growth" (1972, p. 116).

It could be argued that Sarason and associates increased the likelihood of success for all in the clinic because of their interest in personal learning and growth—an interest that must have been stimulating to others. After all, it can be argued that one must simply get at a high level to give at a high level (Sarason, 1971). Sarason and his colleagues demonstrated their willingness to make themselves vulnerable by having the courage to risk failure.

Giving attention to oneself is part of a third dimension of the aesthetics of creating a setting—establishing priorities. Those who give attention to the creation of settings quickly realize that clients in a setting are less a creation of leaders in the setting than of the setting itself. For example, the child in a classroom responds to something larger than the teacher—namely, the setting, which has its own life. Recognizing this helps curriculum leaders give first priority to the entire setting as an influencing body. How strange it sometimes seems that the rhetoric in our folklore and myths in education lead us to believe that one person as leader, such as the principal, teacher, or chief administrator, makes *all* the difference in relating to the client. In fact, the personality of the setting is usually more powerful than the personality of the individual.

Part of priority setting is realizing that a leader involved in creating a setting can't reach everyone in an effective way. One is reminded of the statement of an administrator who gave the commencement address to graduating physicians: "Eighty percent of those patients who come to your office will be fine, regardless of what you do; ten percent are terminally ill and you should do whatever possible to make their last days comfortable ones; and ten percent need critical diagnosis, for their welfare depends on you as a physician; the difficulty is in knowing which patient falls into which group." Indeed, this is a difficulty, but knowing that you, the curriculum leader, are not and cannot be the be-all and end-all for each person in the setting removes a heavy burden—a self-imposed one—from your shoulders. You will not have to pretend to yourself and others that you are a superman or superwoman.

Emphasis on self-understanding and growth in the creation of settings process should not be taken to mean selfishness. The curriculum leader's relationships with others—all consequences of leadership—are an important aspect of the aesthetics of creating a setting. The attention we have given to kinds of covenants and duration of covenants was meant to convey the importance of social intercourse. The elements of trust, autonomy, and initiative are positive results of rich and varied social intercourse.

A sense of playfulness is another dimension of the aesthetics of creating a setting. The curriculum leader as artist will convey the same kind of zest that an artist communicates through art forms such as painting, music, and drama (Brubaker, 1979). Unfortunately, our culture has commanded us to view work and play as discrete processes, as evidenced in our language: workbooks, playgrounds, work areas, play areas, and the like. The curriculum leader as a creator of settings will thoroughly immerse him- or herself in the creative process, so that work and play are integrated. Any distinction between them will become blurred.

As stated earlier in this book, there seems to be a real hunger on the part of educators in a technical society for the openness and just plain fun that we often experienced as children (Brubaker, 1982b). This was brought to my attention recently in a conversation with a superintendent of schools in a large school system. Our time together began as a ritual in which we talked about something outside of ourselves—tasks that needed to be performed so that the staff development experiences we were planning would be successful. As is often the case with such rituals, the tone of the exchange was polite, businesslike, and rather bland. Near the end of the conversation, the superintendent came to life and said,

> You know what really amazes me when I think about where I might go with the remainder of my career and try to be more self-actualized? I wonder how all of this happened. As I look back at my quick moves from teacher to assistant principal to principal to superintendent in three schools systems and think about my humble beginnings, I ask myself, "How did all of this happen?"

The first thing I noted about the superintendent's comments was that they were driven by a sense of awe, wonder, and amazement (Fox, 1983). His imagination and playfulness were evident in his eyes, an intensity of voice, and a forward movement of his head. His total being said, "I am alive with this challenge." As Robert Bly points out, "If we choose 'the one precious thing' . . . the inner King in us that has been asleep for so many years wakes up" (Bly, 1990, p. 177). The superintendent didn't say, I have a problem, and what is the most efficient way to solve it? He embraced the mystery of his upward mobility and wanted to understand it. He didn't engage himself in compulsive busyness, often designed to eliminate or set aside awe, wonder, and amazement. It was as if he had stopped the elevator at one of the upper floors, looked out the window, and seen a garden. He wanted to make sense out of how he got to this floor, and he wondered what it would be like to spend more time tending the garden. (*Self-actualization* was the term he used to identify the garden.)

The lesson for us as creative curriculum leaders interested in the aesthetics of creating settings is obvious: Use the celebration of the creative process as a starting point. As William James expressed it, "Man's chief difference from the brutes lies in the exuberant excess of his subjective propensities. . . . Prune down his extravagances, sober him, and you undo him" (James, 1979, p. 224).

It is hoped that our discussion of the aesthetics of creating a setting will stimulate you to think about the challenge in this area to you as a creative curriculum leader. In the process, you will probably be led into the humanities, such as art, music, drama, and dance. It will be your challenge to integrate the spirit of the artist with the spirit of the scientist, for such an integration is essential for creative curriculum leadership in the twenty-first century. M. Scott Peck (1993) captures this integration in his own leadership experience:

> I keep referring to the integration of task and process as an art as well as a skill. Should you ever have the opportunity to observe a mature community doing it even relatively well, not only will you see civility or organizational behavior in its highest form but you will also witness a human phenomenon of great beauty. (p. 344)

CONCLUSION

Creative curriculum leadership is more difficult and challenging than top-down, manipulative leadership that in effect uses others for the gains of the person in the higher position of authority. The main payoff, however, for the creative curriculum leader and others is the sense of curiosity, awe, wonder, and amazement associated with the learning process. In short, the leader as learner makes all of the difference in creating community.

Case 9: Your Response to a Speech by a Feminist Educator

You are a second-year teacher whose relationship with your teaching mentor can best be described as excellent. You are like-minded on important views of teaching and social issues in general. As luck would have it, both of you are seeking jobs for the following year and think it would be great if you could find jobs in the same school.

You and your mentor decide to visit a nearby university to hear an educator's feminist critique of schools and schooling. The feminist speaker begins by saying that it is generally acknowledged that teaching is a feminized profession, whereas educational administration is not. In effect, the feminist continues, this places positional authority in schools and school systems in the hands of men. It does not make sense, according to the feminist speaker, to add on the feminist perspective, for in effect this simply reinforces the masculine Industrial Age metaphor of the man in the driver's seat. Subject matter within disciplines, educational and occupational hierarchies with their gender-driven division of labor (men in administration and women in teaching), and other male-dominated mechanisms supporting the status quo are the result of adding on the feminist critique, rather than starting afresh with a new view as to what schools and schooling can and should be. The feminist speaker concludes by saying that all of you, men and women, who support the status quo will relegate women to the same role that nurses have played in relation to doctors, and in the process both women and men will be dehumanized.

The speaker, a bright, dynamic, and articulate person, has given you and your cooperating teacher plenty to think about. What will your reaction be as you search for a teaching position, and what will your advice be to your mentor? Please choose the best of the following alternatives:

1. You and your friend should seek a school with a principal, male or female, who has a similar view of what is wrong with schools and schooling and what needs to be done to make things right.

2. Choose a school whose principal is a good leader and manager without regard to his or her views on feminism.

Case 9: Rationales for the Alternative Responses

1. The first thing you should do is give thanks for a genuine friendship. You have established a covenant that is both long lasting and intense. Such relationships are rare in

today's world and can lead to high quality of life at home and at school. The issue of relations between genders in regard to leadership is a highly significant one and should be a major consideration in your choice of a school and its principal. Not to give attention to this issue is to bury your head in the sand. Do your homework and find a principal who will set the tone for the school's culture in a morally responsible way. This is probably the best answer.

2. It is indeed wise to value your good relationship with your friend and mentor, for such covenants are indeed rare. But the principal's role is almost completely that of a manager. It is important that you and your friend have a school that runs smoothly. Issues, such as relations between genders, are of little consequence compared with effective teaching. The problem with this response is that the role of principal is defined in a purely technical way, without regard to value and moral dimensions. How can you teach democracy without giving attention to such dimensions? Consider a better response.

Case 10: A Shared Decision-Making Proposal

Your school year begins with a three-day retreat. Principals in the school system recently attended a conference on a shared decision-making model. They agreed that each school in the system should be invited to apply for pilot or experimental status in moving to a shared decision-making model.

Some reservations are raised about shared decision making at the conference, although all agree that there are drawbacks with the traditional top-down way of exercising authority in organizations in a new Information Age society. In addition, all agree that facilitative power has real potential for professional decision making on the part of teachers and administrators. Facilitative power, according to one principal at the conference, is one way to overcome both obvious and not-so-obvious areas of disagreement in the school. (By facilitative power, this principal means that you bring out the leadership qualities of others, rather than giving them commands.)

The main drawback discussed at the conference is that some principals can misuse shared decision making. Specifically, a principal can blame shared decision-making committee members for his or her own mistakes. It is also true that ultimately the principal at each school is the formally designated leader responsible for the school.

What will your reaction be to the invitation to have your school become a pilot project for shared decision making? Please choose the best of the following options:

1. Give leadership to not supporting shared decision making in your school.

2. Give leadership to supporting shared decision making in your school.

3. Let things take their course. Either way is fine.

Case 10: Rationales for the Alternative Responses

1. Shared decision making, the essence of the shared decision-making model, is a misnomer. There is always one formally designated leader in the school—the principal. If he or she is expected to suspend his or her positional authority, that positional authority can always be returned at a moment's notice. All committees in a school are simply advisory, with real power in the hands of the principal. To pretend otherwise is deceitful. A weak principal can forget his or her role, and the faculty and perhaps the students can take over the school. Chaos will then reign. Be wary of mechanisms that quickly promise change. The quick fix doesn't work. Also, if shared decision making is put in place, faculty will be expected to enter into an intense and long-range covenant with one another and the principal. You are hired to teach, not administer the school. All of these arguments hold in some schools where shared decision making has been misused. If, however, your school has teachers with leadership potential and interest in shared decision making, this method has real potential. To reject the proposal out of hand for a pilot project is a mistake. Consider other alternatives.

2. The invitation to apply for pilot status in the new shared decision-making program has tremendous potential for effecting change in the school. Facilitative power is clearly consistent with societal changes in general, and with the move from an Industrial Age to an Information Age society in particular. It is also a sign of hope that professionalism can be enhanced and a sense of community can be increased in the school. This does introduce the probability of an intense covenant of considerable duration, but the payoff can be significant. You must be alert, however, to the possibility that the principal, who is formally designated as the final authority in the school, can take back at any moment the power shared with teachers. If such an event occurs, you and your colleagues must know how to use other sources of power to achieve your goals. In conclusion, there is the real possibility of creating a Win–Win climate in your school. Go for it.

3. There are advantages to not getting involved. You won't be blamed if things go wrong, and you can hang around the edges, thus saving your resources, such as time, energy, and expertise. Nonetheless, the move toward shared decision making has gone too far to simply play a passive role. This "Win–Win or No Deal" way of relating to colleagues and the principal will in effect keep you out of the school arena. You will not accept your professional responsibility by taking this stance, and you could well convey the feeling that you are either uninterested or too good to get involved. Seek a better response.

Case 11: Testing Irregularities Are Reported to You

You are a respected educator in a medium-sized school system. You have received a letter from a parent volunteer who spends a good deal of time in an elementary school. The letter contains the following comments:

There has been a good deal of coverage of testing irregularities (cheating) on television (e.g., on shows such as "60 Minutes") and in newspapers.

Since I love my job as a parent volunteer, I must remain anonymous and trust you to ensure this.

However, I have been an actual witness to the following things as teachers have given the C.A.T. (California Achievement Test):

1. Stopping midtest to teach something coming up on the test that the students had not been taught

2. Before handing in the tests given that day, looking ahead to copy down the upcoming test questions and teaching them verbatim

3. Tapping a child on the shoulder to point out an incorrect answer and giving him the A-OK sign when he erased it and filled in the correct answer

4. Going overtime

5. Allowing children to go back and finish up previous sections that they had not completed within the time limit

6. Reading the directions more than once to the children or paraphrasing them to emphasize what the teacher especially wanted the children to know

7. Allowing the children to have little math-fact cheat cards on their desks that they could refer to during the test, because they never learned math facts on their own

What will you do? Please choose the best of the following alternatives:

1. Share the letter with the proper authorities in the school system.

2. Share the letter with the proper authorities in the school system and follow up to be sure that action has been taken.

3. Ignore the letter.

Case 11: Rationales for the Alternative Responses

1. Cheating cannot be condoned, but must be put in the context of modern society. Unrelenting emphasis on high achievement test scores has reached epidemic proportions, with cheating the natural result. Our society has supported the Win–Lose norm, with many parents doing whatever is necessary for their children to get special advantage over

other children. Assigned readings are stolen from university libraries so that premed and prelaw students receive higher grades that will give them special advantage to get into medical and law schools. Many parents pressure their children to learn to read before they reach kindergarten. Some parents do whatever is necessary to give their children special advantage in becoming members of cheerleading and athletic teams. Cheating is not only wrong but also contaminates the test score results of students who have done well on tests without cheating. Share the letter with proper authorities in your school system. All of the above is true, but stops short of informing you as to what will happen, if anything, once the letter has been shared with authorities. Search for a better alternative.

2. The response to this matter described in Alternative 1 is necessary but insufficient. The issues the letter raises are so important that you must not only report the matter to authorities, such as the director of testing and the superintendent(s), but also be sure that appropriate action is taken, including the retesting of the classes involved and appropriate punishment of the culpable teachers. You may well experience some difficulties and pain as you give resources to this matter, but the issues involved are significant enough to endure a high level of commitment.

3. Not getting involved will conserve your resources in the short run, but you will not be meeting your professional responsibilities by hiding your head in the sand. Find a better response.

Case 12: New Principal States Intention to Ignore History and Culture of the School

Recent years have been difficult for you in your school. The recently released principal had a leadership style that divided the faculty on a number of key issues. As a result, the superintendent of schools has recommended and the board of education has appointed a new principal from another state.

During the fall orientation meeting of the faculty, the new principal says the following: "It is time for a fresh start for all of us in this school. I don't want any of you to come to me with stories about past difficulties. Let us begin as if this is a brand-new school with brand-new faculty members."

What will you do in reaction to the new principal's comments? Please choose the best of the following alternatives:

1. Ignore the new principal's comments.

2. Remind yourself that the history and culture of the school are a significant variable in decision making at the present time and make this known to the faculty and principal at the orientation meeting for the faculty.

3. The history and culture of the school are important to keep in mind as present decisions are made. You must find a better time, however, probably in a private conversation with the principal, to share your view with the principal.

Case 12: Rationales for the Alternative Responses

1. Once again, to ignore the matter will conserve your resources in the short run and keep you out of trouble, but the new principal's position is important enough that you will not be meeting your professional responsibilities by doing nothing. Choose a better option.

2. You are right to give attention to the history and culture of the setting, and to address this matter directly, at the front end of your relationship with the new principal. Thus he or she and the faculty will know that you are willing to act on your beliefs. The difficulty with this response is that the new principal is trying to establish his or her credibility with the faculty for the first time in an official setting at the first faculty meeting. Your outspoken action will leave him or her little room to save face. Seek a better alternative.

3. Some action on your part needs to be taken. In the decision-making process, your new principal and other school leaders must take into account the history and culture of the setting. The best time to deal with this issue is in a one-on-one conversation with the new principal. This way, you will not be openly challenging the new principal in a formal setting.

7

Civility in Leadership

The Ultimate Difference

Civility is hardly the only way to live, but it is the only way that is worthwhile.

—M. Scott Peck (1993, p. 54)

Effective citizenship has been a major goal of public education in the United States since its inception (Brubaker, 1967). The teaching of civics was viewed as the mechanism for inculcating proper values in the young. The very health of democratic society was perceived to be at stake as schools geared up to meet this challenge. Public commitment is evidenced by self-imposed taxation. The word *civility* sounds much like civics, with the former usually linked to manners and politeness, those small behaviors that tend to make others like us (Peck, 1993). The civil leader sometimes does things that don't win the approval of others, however. M. Scott Peck refers to an amusing but profound quote from Oliver Herford: "A gentleman is one who never hurts anyone's feelings unintentionally" (Peck, 1993). In other words, manners and politeness are moral behaviors if they increase our consciousness of the preciousness of each person and the relationship of self, others, and organizations on behalf of this humanistic tradition (Peck, 1993).

When manners and politeness are invoked to simply get the approval of others, they are self-serving and as such usually don't have the ring of authenticity and integrity. When manners and politeness are used in this way, they communicate the leader's desire to avoid all pain, and yet maintaining the health of a person or organization is often a painful process (Peck, 1993).

An example of pain that often accompanies civility is described best by a third-grade teacher who has recently been losing sleep and weight:

> Each school in our system has a report card that tells the public our annual goal, objectives, and plan of action. Our school's major goal was to raise standardized test scores. My class was well on its way to meeting this goal when a new student, a nonreader with low test scores, arrived on the scene from another town. My first reaction was "Why did I have to get this student? I wish he would move again!" At the same time I realized that I, a good teacher, was exactly the kind of person who could make a difference in his life. (Brubaker & Simon, 1993, p. 19)

How did the third-grade teacher reconcile this contradiction? First, she was conscious of the pain she was experiencing and recognized that her devotion to a higher authority than self—the preciousness of the child—was more important than appearing to be a winner with higher test scores. Second, she decided to do the work necessary to deal with this situation, rather than denying its reality. Without being conscious of it, she located her commitment to the child and situation at Level 5, and perhaps Level 4, on the following Commitment Scale/Hierarchy (Brubaker & Nelson, 1974, p. 102):

1. I will sacrifice my life and/or the lives of my family and/or those I dearly love.

2. I will give up the respect of those whom I love and I'll forego my status and professional achievement.

3. I will forego economic security and my career.

4. I will have serious conflicts between what I think should be done and my reluctance to do it. I may have to alter my work style and give up those techniques that had previously been successful and beneficial and learn new ones.

5. I will have to alter some habits with which I'm quite comfortable, thus making my job somewhat more difficult. I will feel uncomfortable from time to time because I'll do things that don't seem to be the best way to do them based on my past experience and present assumptions.

6. It doesn't make any difference as past experience indicates. My choice, therefore, is between Tweedledum and Tweedledee.

Did the teacher know that she would intentionally hurt the feelings of the principal, superintendent of schools, and school board? Yes. Her actions were conscious and deliberate. But she was simply committed to a lateral rather than a hierarchical relationship with her organization, the school, and the school system (Peck, 1993). She had made a civil commitment in response to an incivility pressure to achieve high test scores so that adult educators would appear to be winners. In fact, we could well say that her bias for children worked in her favor. William Buckley (1982) underscores how bias can be a kind of advantage: "Ken Galbraith and I have in common what strikes some as a disadvantage, but isn't: namely our plainspoken bias, which gives a harnessing energy to our work" (p. 239).

A second example relates to my moving to the South more than twenty years ago. A colleague who had lived in the state all of his life counseled me on one of the major civilities of the region: "We don't go anywhere where we aren't wanted." I asked him about the civil rights sit-ins that had occurred in Greensboro, and heard a reply that demonstrated no connection between *civil* rights and African American students not being served at the lunch counter. The sit-ins literally placed themselves at Level 1 of the Commitment Scale/Hierarchy in defiance of traditional southern manners and politeness.

Perhaps the main benefit in exercising your civil rights is to yourself. In February 1986, Anatoli Shcharansky (1986)

Soviet Jew, dissident, and accused American spy was released from a Soviet prison, sent to Israel, and freedom, after nine years in custody. His weight had varied from 81 to 165 pounds. He had become not only a powerful voice of dissent in the Soviet Union but also a bridge between Soviet Jewry and the rest of the human rights movement. When he was asked about his time in prison, he responded as follows:

> You are punished if you write to the authorities on behalf of another prisoner—say a sick man who is not getting any medical attention. The authorities say, "Look, your letters don't help." And they are logically right. But there exists another, inner logic: the prisoner who writes such a letter may not save his neighbor in the next cell, but he saves his soul. (p. 38)

A METAPHOR FOR SCHOOLS

It is interesting to hear school administrators and teachers use metaphors to describe their schools. The most frequently used metaphor is that of the family. As M. Scott Peck (1993) has noted, the primary role of a family is to nurture its members. It is true that nurturing is a major role of effective principals and assistant principals. Yet the family metaphor doesn't hold in other respects. Principals hire and fire teachers and other staff members, for example. These functions are more accurately associated with a business. In Robert Frost's poem, "The Death of the Hired Man," the husband, a farmer, says, "Home is the place where, when you have to go there, they have to take you in" (Peck, 1993, p. 196).

Another difficulty with the family metaphor for schools is that it is easy to conceive of them as patriarchies or matriarchies, where the principal is in effect a benevolent or not-so-benevolent parent. Teachers and other staff members can, through transference, "a neurotic and uncivil distortion of reality," continue to relate to their new "father" or "mother" in positive or negative ways (Peck, 1993, p. 214).

In recent years, a more apt metaphor for a school is that of a business. Test scores and other number-related products are marketed by some teachers, principals, superintendents, and school board members (Peck, 1993). Testing irregularities, that euphemism for cheating, are a side effect as teachers and administrators want to appear to be winners. In some cases, teachers and others are given permission to cheat. In other cases, administrators are so focused on raising test scores that they simply don't give attention to testing irregularities.

At any rate, the creative curriculum leader can use the concept of metaphors as a way to discuss with teachers and others which metaphors promote true civility and which do not. There is obviously no one right answer to this question.

THE TABLE MANNERS OF LEADERSHIP AND DEVELOPING YOUR OWN CURRICULUM

When I was a child, I was asked—perhaps told is a better way to say it—to set the table before dinner. My immediate inclination was to resist the order, but I discovered with time that there was a sense of security and order in this task, something that gave me the feeling I was making an important contribution to the dinner hour.

What I didn't realize at the time was that this table manner was one of several that set the stage for good conversation among family members. (How foreign this sounds to a generation that has learned to throw dinner on a TV tray and head for the den.) The dinner hour was a time to exchange information and feelings, a time to converse and listen. In short, it was a time to learn from each other.

As an adult I came to see the importance of what Roland Nelson, at the Center for Creative Leadership in Greensboro, North Carolina, calls the "table manners of leadership." By this he means those small behaviors that facilitate an exchange of information and feelings that lead to learning and better relationships. Stated another way, the table manners of leadership are not used to manipulate people as objects within a bureaucratic hierarchy (Peck, 1993). Rather, they are used to create environments (curricula) where persons can learn from each other in lateral relationships. In the remainder of this section of the chapter, I discuss the table manners of leadership within school settings that can stimulate learning and better relationships among all within these environments. In the process, the leader and others can develop their own curricula.

Entrance and exit rituals are important in any setting. For example, one of the adages in the luxury hotel business is "that if you manage the first and last impressions of a guest properly, then you'll have a happy guest" (Kleinfield, 1989, p. 36). One of the first things hotel workers are told is that eye contact is a necessary behavior for greeting guests when they arrive at the hotel (Kleinfield, 1989). Such contact communicates your willingness to go out of your way to help the person(s) entering the setting, and it says you are risking a certain kind of vulnerability on their behalf.

It has always been amazing to me to watch some leaders use smiles and other nonverbal behaviors to relax persons entering a setting. They also frequently exhibit the ability to establish an affinity connection with so-called small talk.

Leaders who have given attention to entrance rituals know the importance of the physical setting. For example, one school principal inherited a high counter that served as a barrier between guests and the secretary. The counter was removed to facilitate exchange of ideas and feelings. Another principal instructed the secretary and others to always begin conversations with guests by saying, "Welcome to *our* school. How may I help you?"

A good energy level on the part of the greeter is important, but it is not sufficient in itself. Guests want to know that school leaders have a sense of purpose so that children and adults will be involved in meaningful activity. A clear but concise vision statement communicates this sense of direction: "Everything we do here is aimed at helping children and adults become the best they can be." This general vision statement can be followed by more specific goals for the school.

Principals and others who serve as greeters may profit from knowing the difference between acceptable onstage and backstage behaviors. For example, the person who is counting lunch money would do well to do so in the principal's office rather than in the secretaries' area. This responsibility requires uninterrupted concentration. If the person in charge of counting money considers guests to be an interruption, then guests will not feel invited into the school. It is good to remind ourselves that some chaos backstage is necessary for an orderly environment onstage (Kleinfield, 1989).

Exit rituals are equally significant. For example, the principal and other adult educators who walk parents and other guests to the door have the opportunity to prolong their conversation and demonstrate their care for the guests. It is an opportunity to summarize what has happened during the visit, thank guests for their interest in the children and the school, and invite them back for another visit.

Exit rituals have demonstrated repeatedly that there is no more loyal guest than one who has a problem that gets fixed (Kleinfield, 1989, p. 32). Luxury hotel surveys have also revealed time and again "that guests very much like being called by name" (Kleinfield, 1989, p. 35).

Listening is probably the most powerful civility available to the creative curriculum leader. It is flattering to the speaker and it demonstrates that you aren't self-centered, but instead are eager to learn more about the person speaking. By focusing on the speaker, you will also lessen your anxiety (Linver, 1978). By actively listening, you will communicate that you understand where the speaker is coming from and care enough about that person to step into his or her shoes (Linver, 1978). Make no mistake about it, listening is hard work, what M. Scott Peck has called a manifestation of love (Peck, 1978). It relies on the discipline of bracketing, "the temporary giving up or setting aside of one's own prejudices, frames of reference, and desires" (Peck, 1978, p. 128). The true listener temporarily communicates total acceptance of the speaker, the result being that the person speaking will feel less threatened and will make himself or herself more vulnerable by telling you more (Peck, 1978).

It is clear from our discussion of the table manners of leadership that the effective leader primarily sees self as learner. The curiosity the effective leader has about other persons, self, and organizational settings will be a driving force in his or her own curriculum development. Growth and learning will oftentimes be their own reward—benefits that far outweigh money and possessions.

Speaking is another critical communicative skill that may be important in learning more about yourself and others.

How significant is this skill in comparison to writing? Sandy Linver (1978), author of the best-selling book *Speakeasy*, answers this question: "The way we interact with other people both personally and professionally, has very little to do with the written word. It is almost totally based on speaking" (p. 18).

There is no one right speaking style. Rather, a speaker's credibility depends on authenticity or genuineness. It therefore makes sense that the starting place for good speaking is to know what kind of person you basically are.

Please take a moment to complete the following self-inventory. It will give you a start in assessing your comfort and proficiency as a speaker.

Table 7.1 *How Good (and Comfortable) Are You as a Public Speaker?*

Please assess your comfort and proficiency on the following items, from 1 (*low*) to 5 (*high*):

	Comfort	Proficiency
1. Speaking one-to-one.		
2. Listening one-to-one.		
3. Answering questions one-to-one.		
4. Speaking to a small group.		
5. Listening (as the speaker/leader) to verbal and nonverbal language of the group.		
6. Answering questions after speaking to a small group.		
7. Speaking to a large group.		
8. Listening (as the speaker/leader) to verbal and nonverbal language in a large group.		
9. Answering questions after speaking to a large group.		
10. Telephone interviews.		
11. Television interviews.		
12. Radio interviews.		
13. Newspaper reporter interviews.		

Are you more comfortable relating to people in formal or informal situations? If your style is more formal, use a podium and stick closely to your detailed notes or written speech. If your style is more informal, push the lectern aside and move into the audience as if you were having a conversation. Once again, draw on your "honesty and courage to be authentic with your audience and project to them who you really are" (Linver, 1978, p. 59). One of the best examples of authentic responses was reported in *Time* magazine on January 4, 1993 (p. 55). Television brought the devastation of the Los Angeles riots into every living room, and an unsophisticated man nervously stepped before the camera and said, "Can we all get along?" It was the TV moment of the year.

Regardless of your style, the secret is to focus on the audience, rather than yourself, and share your warmth with them. One good way to focus on the audience is to think about how curious you are to learn more about them and their reaction to your ideas. You will discover that it's this desire for contact, to make something happen, that gives a speaker energy (Linver, 1978, p. 41). One way to share your warmth is to share your sense of humor. This has the effect of relaxing the audience, whether it is one person or one hundred.

My father attended a college alumni meeting in Bradenton, Florida, hundreds of miles away from his alma mater, Albion College, in Michigan. The speaker was the president of the college. My father called me after the speech and raved about the president. "Why did you like him so much?" I asked. Dad responded, "He talked to each of us before the speech about our personal interests in the college, and he cared about what we had to say." In short, the president set the stage for his own success before he even spoke a word in the more formal setting. In the process, the president relaxed himself before the speech.

The physical setting in which you speak sets the stage for your speaking. In both formal and informal settings, it can be useful to have a mental checklist. For example, remove distractions, such as a gurgling coffeepot; have chairs and tables arranged the way you want them; assess acoustics and check equipment; and have a copy of your resume for the person who is introducing you. Your preparation for the situation sends the message "I care enough about you, the audience, to have done my homework." Good preparation also gives you, the speaker, a sense of security.

In many situations, you will naturally be nervous to some extent before speaking. Treat this nervousness as a good thing, for it means that you care enough about the audience and yourself to get psyched up for the occasion. Self-talk can be helpful as you prepare: "Good going. I have an edge on and I know that this is necessary in order to do a good job." It is especially helpful to realize that the audience wants you to succeed and is therefore with you from the start.

As related throughout this book, the audience wants to know what your personal curriculum is and how you have developed it. They want to know where you have been, where you are, and where you want to go in the future. In short, for the audience, *you are the curriculum*. There will obviously be areas of mutual concern if not common experiences. In speaking to this mutuality, you will establish an affinity connection.

One of the advantages that speaking has over writing is that you get immediate reaction to your ideas. Because 65 percent of communication is nonverbal body language, you will be able to read your audience and know how your ideas are being received. As you share your warmth with them, they will share their warmth with you.

Because more and more educators are expected to go on television, I have prepared a list of guidelines for this challenge:

1. Talk to the reporter, not the camera or microphone. (Look the reporter straight in the eye.)

2. Stand or sit erectly. Don't stoop or bend over.

3. If you say "No comment," add that you will get back to the reporter by such and such a time.

4. Know who you're dealing with and develop rapport with the reporter when possible.

5. Remember that the good photographer (cameraperson) doesn't always have the camera to his or her eye. The camera can be rolling from any position, even if it is under his or her arm.

6. Be politely on guard all of the time.

7. Take advantage of nonconfrontational good news programs.

8. The bottom line is to meet reporters head-on and be honest. The camera doesn't lie. It will see the eyes.

9. Be cool and confident. It disarms reporters.

10. Remember that there is a high degree of sensitivity about minorities and women at this time in the history of our nation.

11. A smile is the most disarming thing in the world. Bring to the camera the real person inside you.

12. Be prepared. If you don't know, say, "I don't know."

13. There is no such thing as "off the record." Beware of the reporter who says, "This is off-the-record."

14. You can ask to talk to the reporter about something before you go on camera. If the reporter won't allow you to do this, don't talk.

15. It is a good idea to suggest a place for the interview. Get an appropriate visual backdrop.

16. Watch hazards around you. Don't swivel in a chair. Don't fidget. Calm down, even if it means that you grab a desk in front of you or behind you.

17. Take your time.

18. Ask to reshoot if you are extremely dissatisfied with the interview.

19. Limit the number of remarks and focus on two or three major points.

20. Ask the reporter both whom he or she has talked to and whom he or she will talk to before the story is over.

21. You can occasionally stop a reporter dead in his or her tracks by saying, "I have no earthly idea what you're talking about."

22. The school or central office is private property. Be aware, however, that television cameras can shoot onto your property from a nearby site without your permission.

Familiarity with television interviews will be enhanced as you have more and more experiences with reporters. How does one get better and better at this? Practice, practice, practice. "Winston Churchill was asked what he did in his spare time. He responded, 'I rehearse my extemporaneous speeches'" (Adams, 1983, p. 229).

Writing affords you another vehicle for communicating with parents and others interested in schools. Time and time again, parents share with others memos from the principal's office that have serious spelling and grammatical errors. Teachers' comments on student papers also sometimes have such errors. Parents ask, "How can they teach good writing when they don't know what good writing is?"

Correct spelling and grammar are important table manners of leadership. Because we all make spelling and grammatical errors, the secret is to have a proficient copy editor who will proofread memos and the like. It takes extra effort and time to use a proofreader, but many an embarrassing moment can be avoided with such effort.

An important question to ask in sending a letter or memorandum is, "What is my purpose in doing this?" This purpose should be clearly stated, with concrete next steps spelled out concisely and precisely, so that the parents or other adults know what they are expected to do in response to your communication. In the event that you want to be sure of and expedite a response from an individual, include a stamped, self-addressed envelope.

Finally, always send clean copy. Poorly typed communications and badly photocopied materials send the message that you are sloppy and unprofessional.

Miscellaneous table manners of creative curriculum leadership are as follows:

1. When leaving a message on a telephone answering machine, state your name, telephone number, nature of the business, and the best time to return the call. *State this information slowly.* Remember, the person listening to your request is writing the information down.

2. Before meeting with other persons or having important phone conversations, prepare for the content of the

conversation, even if this means writing notes from which you speak.

3. Always give your full name when making a phone call. Many people begin speaking, and the other party has no idea who it is.

4. There are two major ways to ensure that you can do something with the support of your bureaucratic superiors: (a) remove irritants and (b) be willing to share the credit if efforts are successful, and share the blame if they are not.

5. When you arrive at substantive agreements over the telephone, follow up with a memorandum of understanding, concluding with, "Unless I hear from you otherwise, I'll assume this is correct."

6. Log important contacts with other parties.

7. Remember that seemingly private e-mails may become public.

We would do well to remind ourselves that all forms of communication are promissory activity (Goffman, 1959). We promise that we will act out what we have said we will do. We will, as they say these days, walk the talk. In more sophisticated academic terms, we will involve ourselves in praxis: reflective action.

CONCLUSION

The details of creative curriculum leadership, such as the table manners of leadership, are a necessary but insufficient part of the leader's civility. When such details are part of the leader's total character, we gauge the effectiveness of the whole person. I have argued in this book that highly effective leaders view others as precious human beings, whose talents can be identified and used in the creation of settings and organizations. This does not mean that leaders and others always agree. It does mean that they relate to each other with honesty, integrity, and authenticity.

Case 13: Some Upper-Middle-Class Parents Fight to Keep Tracking

After reviewing relevant research and consulting within the field, the new superintendent of schools worked with her staff to design a plan to move the schools away from their system of tracking students. Opposition to this plan began to surface when the school board held hearings on the subject. This opposition was primarily located in the upper-middle-class neighborhoods in general and the country clubs in particular. The bottom line for these parents is that they wanted their children to be in classes with "the nice people"—that is, people whom they believe are like themselves. They perceive their children as having special advantages for entrance into college and the like if tracking is retained.

You have been appointed to a committee of K–12 educators in your system whose members serve to advise the superintendent on this matter. What will your advice be? Please choose the best of the following alternatives:

1. Advise the superintendent to hold firm and implement her plan to move the schools away from the system of tracking students.

2. Advise the superintendent to withdraw the plan for moving the schools away from the system of tracking students.

3. Stay out of the battle. Say and do nothing.

Case 13: Rationales for the Alternative Responses

1. Tracking is antidemocratic: The rich get richer and the poor get poorer. Those who support tracking want a special advantage for their children. The superintendent is correct in her review of relevant research, for such research doesn't support tracking. In fact, more students learn more content in classes in which tracking doesn't take place.

2. Ability grouping keeps the gifted students from being cheated by accommodating individual differences and scholastic aptitude. Ability grouping is especially important

in English, mathematics, science, and languages. Urge the superintendent of schools to withdraw her proposal to eliminate tracking. Support the upper-middle-class parents who lead the opposition to the superintendent. Because these parents have more experience in using the sources of power known as expertise, charisma, and succor, they can have greater influence on those with positional authority—namely, the school board. In addition, these parents have mastered the use of the table manners of leadership (civilities) and can use them to get what they want. The difficulties with this response are several: Research doesn't support the continuation of tracking; access to higher-level classes is limited for persons from lower socioeconomic classes; and the favored have a feeling of entitlement. Therefore, consider other responses to find a better alternative.

3. Not getting involved does conserve your resources. You also will not get hurt if the battle heats up. Nonetheless, you abdicate your professional responsibilities by not taking a stand. Seek a better response. (Note: See the Commitment Scale Hierarchy at the beginning of this chapter.)

Case 14: You Are Asked to Assess a Star Teacher on Your Team

You are new to the school and are asked to join a team of teachers. On your team there is a veteran teacher whom the principal and many teachers at the school treat as a star. You notice that the teacher's stardom is the result of several factors: The teacher sings in the church choir of a leading church in the city and is a leader in that church; the teacher volunteers for many committees in the school system and serves as the central office's demonstration teacher for workshops; the teacher dresses well; and the teacher has excellent public relations skills with parents and others in the community.

You also notice, however, that the teacher almost never teaches. That is, the teacher writes assignments on the board that keep the students busy but rarely teaches the subject matter content and does not grade the students' work in completing the assignments. The star teacher does not record grades in the grade book but instead gives the students nothing lower than a C, even though many of the students do not know the material and should receive low or failing marks. Parents do not complain because their children get good grades.

The star teacher recently won the school system's Teacher of the Year award, which consisted of a certificate, press coverage, and $5,000. Last year, she was a finalist for the Language Arts Teacher of the Year award, although language arts was taught only three times during the year—on the days the teacher was observed by the central office language arts consultant.

The star teacher is currently up for the Social Studies Teacher of the Year award. The only time social studies was taught during the first six months of the school year was the day the principal did the formal evaluation of the teacher. On that day, the teacher reached into the cupboard and distributed Native American costumes that the children used to act out a role-playing exercise.

The social studies consultant from the central office asks you to come to the central office to give testimony that will be useful in assessing the star teacher's performance.

What will your response be? Please choose from the following alternatives:

1. Simply say to the consultant that you don't have enough information to respond.

2. Assess the star teacher by only applauding her polite behaviors and public relations skills—in other words, what most people consider civilities.

3. Give an honest evaluation of the star teacher, including all of the backstage behaviors you have observed.

Case 14: Rationales for the Alternative Responses

1. It is true that you won't help or hurt the star teacher, but you won't have assumed professional responsibility in the process. You will conserve your resources of time and energy by not getting involved, but the price is too high. Consider other responses.

2. By focusing on her polite behaviors and public relations skills, you will be telling part of the story and will not

hurt the teacher's chances for another award. After all, she is only hurting herself in doing what she does. There have been no checks in place, including those the principal could have put there, in the past. This teacher's civilities are making the whole school look better because of her many awards. The appearance of being a winner is more important in our society than actually being a winner, and the star teacher is simply reinforcing this norm. The difficulty with this response is that it perpetuates superficiality and incompetence. Consider other responses.

3. An honest assessment may well cause you some difficulties and pain if word of your evaluation reaches other teachers, including the star teacher. That is, you may be operating at Level 4 or Level 5 on the Commitment Scale/Hierarchy, whereas Alternatives 1 and 2 would keep you at Level 6. ("It doesn't make any difference, as past experience indicates. My choice, therefore, is between Tweedledum and Tweedledee.") The payoffs for you in giving an honest assessment are many: (a) You will have the self-esteem that comes with being genuine and doing the right thing, the highest hallmark of civility; (b) you will know that you have been a professional who was willing to censure a colleague, if necessary; and (c) the star teacher will not get an award that would further perpetuate her fraud. This is the best response.

Case 15: You Sense a Need for Faculty and Students to Learn the Table Manners of Leadership

You are a veteran teacher with a high level of credibility among colleagues. You are on the principal's advisory council and the lead teacher on your teaching team. For some time now, you have been concerned about the lack of table manners of leadership on the part of some teachers on your staff. For example, they don't listen well to colleagues or support their efforts, but rather simply talk about their own accomplishments. And a few literally don't have table manners during the lunch hour in the cafeteria.

The problem is compounded by the fact that these same teachers aren't setting a good example for many of the children in the school. Yet you feel that children have to learn the table manners of leadership if they are to have the chance to succeed in any occupation in life.

What will you do about this matter? Please choose the best of the following alternatives:

1. Go directly to those teachers who have problems in this area of human behavior and, using all of your public relations skills, make your case for improving their table manners of leadership.

2. Talk to the principal about your concerns and see where you go from there.

3. Go directly to the principal's advisory council and make your concerns known.

4. Put the matter aside and concentrate on other matters; this issue is too sensitive to proceed.

Case 15: Rationales for the Alternative Responses

1. This response has all of the virtues of any direct action. You will make your views known to the people who have the problem. The difficulty with this approach is that, naturally, those with the problem will probably resent your judgment and resist your efforts to change their behavior. Consider other alternatives.

2. The principal is the formally designated head of the school and as such would probably want to be involved at the front end of any efforts to deal with this issue. Also, the principal is in a position to make things happen without your communicating a holier-than-thou attitude. In all likelihood, the principal will involve the advisory council, and you will play a key role in setting up workshops or the like to deal with this matter. For example, the whole faculty may be invited to hear a flight attendant speak about the table manners of leadership taught by airlines. An indirect approach, in this case, has more virtues than drawbacks. This is probably the best response.

3. This is a matter of consequence that will ultimately need to be handled by teachers in the school. It is professional courtesy to involve other teachers at the beginning of this

process. There are two major difficulties with this response: (a) The principal will not be involved, thus keeping you from using his or her positional authority at the onset; and (b) colleagues may well feel you are self-righteous or holier than thou, in which case your credibility will be eroded. Consider other responses.

4. Not stating your views on an issue so important to you is a Lose–Win strategy that could well lead to other problems. Specifically, you may release your anger at those with few table manners of leadership in a way that will be detrimental to them and you. Consider better responses.

Case 16: Principal Hears
New Superintendent's Views on Dress

You, a principal, are having lunch with the new superintendent before the school year begins. The superintendent says, "You can't convince me that people don't sense whether you're professional from the minute they see how you're dressed. Good ol' boy principals usually wear short-sleeved shirts, rather than suits or sharp sport coats, and they often wear outdated ties and plaid blazers." Now that you know your new superintendent's views on these matters, how will you act as principal with regard to these views? Choose from the following alternative responses or add a better response of your own.

1. A principal's competence is what counts. Does he or she deliver? Dress is a personal and idiosyncratic matter. Continue to dress as you have and advise fellow principals to do likewise.

2. Make minor adjustments in your dress if they are called for. Advise your colleagues to do likewise.

3. Follow the new superintendent's dress code. Advise your colleagues to do likewise.

Case 16: Rationales for the Alternative Responses

1. Dress is your own business and has nothing to do with success as a principal. You have demonstrated that you have

done the job well and people know that. The products of your work are what's really important. Don't openly confront the superintendent, but go about your business as you always have done.

2. You will be a minor irritant on occasion to the superintendent, but you surely won't get into the trouble that you would get into with the first response. Have clothes that are in style, whenever possible, but dress according to what makes you comfortable as much as you can. Be sure to dress appropriately for big occasions when the superintendent wants to show off the staff to the board and the community. Consider the next alternative.

3. Dressing correctly is a small price to pay for the good results you will achieve. Many people will remember the impression you make with your clothes more than anything else. You are more likely to move up the ladder and be a successful administrator if you follow the superintendent's advice. Dress is symbolic, a kind of emotional shorthand, and as such it becomes an important matter to superintendents as they relate to principals. Superintendents want the organization and themselves to look good and appear to be winners.

Case 17: Superintendent Informed of Principal's Racist and Sexist Humor

A teacher informs you that her principal tells racist, sexist, and dirty jokes to teachers of both genders, in a variety of settings. You have personally observed the principal telling dirty jokes and have also had confirmation of the teacher's charges from others in the central office. What will you do? Choose from these alternative responses or add a better response of your own.

1. Confront the principal and tell him that racist and sexist humor can get him fired, and you want no more of it on his part. Overlook the dirty jokes. Talk to him about these jokes only if you hear another complaint from a person of the opposite sex.

2. Overlook the matter and just go about your business as superintendent of schools.

3. Confront the principal and tell him that racist and sexist humor as well as dirty jokes are inappropriate, illegal under Title IX, and will hurt his or her professional image as well as the image of the school and school system. Follow up with a memorandum that makes your position a matter of public record in the event that you are ever confronted about the matter.

4. Have your assistant superintendent, who works directly with principals, deal with this matter. Be sure you are informed as to how the matter is handled. In this way, you won't experience the downside of being directly involved. That is, the assistant superintendent will be held accountable for the situation.

Case 17: Rationales for the Alternative Responses

1. You are wise to confront the principal so that he gets straight signals on the matter of racist and sexist humor. It can get both of you in trouble and therefore must be addressed immediately. So-called dirty jokes are an affinity connection or kind of male-bonding mechanism. Just be sure that the principal understands that such jokes are not to be told in front of women. Please choose again.

2. People are always complaining about something, and these days they are supersensitive about matters like these. After all, school board members sometimes tell off-color jokes as a way to bond and relax. Please choose again.

3. This is probably the best response. People are naturally more sensitive to issues of racism and sexism, and the courts reflect this sensitivity. All educators must understand that inappropriate humor is simply that. Remember, you are the model for all educators in the system.

4. Delegation of responsibility is the hallmark of an effective superintendent. You shouldn't have to take the heat on all matters, and this matter serves as a case in point. The difficulty is that delegation in this case is in effect a missed opportunity for you to let all principals know your stand on this important matter. The previous response is probably better.

8

Creating Learning Communities

For the first two-thirds of the twentieth century a powerful tide bore Americans into ever deeper engagement in the life of their communities, but a few decades ago—silently, warning—that tide reversed and we were overtaken by a treacherous rip current. Without at first noticing, we have been pulled apart from one another and from our communities over the last third of the century.

—Robert D. Putnam (2000, p. 27)

The creative curriculum leader recognizes the changing nature of communities cited by Robert Putnam, Peter and Isabel Malkin Professor of Public Policy at Harvard University. Putnam draws on vast new data from the Roper Social and Political Trends and the DDB Needham Lifestyle Surveys to demonstrate how we have become increasingly disconnected from family, friends, neighbors, and social structures. The title of his book, *Bowling Alone: The Collapse and Revival of American Community*, vividly illustrates the present state of things in our society. We no longer bowl in leagues. We bowl alone. To bowl alone is to withdraw from community.

Yet Putnam gives us hope that American community can be revived—much as it was at the end of the nineteenth century. He argues that our civic and social life can be replenished.

Putnam asks us to consider the following possible forces behind the slump in civic engagement and social capital:

Busyness and time pressure

Economic hard times

The movement of women into the paid labor force and the stresses of two-career families

Residential mobility

Suburbanization and sprawl

Television, the electronic revolution, and other technological changes

Changes in the structure of the economy, such as the rise of chain stores, branch firms, and the service sector, or globalization

Disruption of marriage and family ties

Growth of the welfare state

The civil rights revolution

The sixties (most of which actually happened in the seventies), including Vietnam, Watergate, and disillusion with public life

The cultural revolt against authority (sex, drugs, and so on) (p. 187)

Interestingly enough, Putnam traces in his book the origin of the key concept, *social capital*, to L. J. Hanifan, state supervisor of rural schools in West Virginia. Writing in 1916, Hanifan (1920), a practical reformer of the Progressive Era, used social capital to refer to "those tangible substances [that] count for most in the daily lives of people: namely goodwill, fellowship, sympathy, and social intercourse among the individuals and families who make up a social unit" (p. 130). He added, "The individual is helpless socially, if left to himself" (p. 130).

The point that Putnam makes with regard to social capital is simply that social networks have value for they create a sense of personal and community efficacy: "I can make a difference and we can make a difference!" Furthermore, Putnam (2000) reminds us that "networks of community engagement foster sturdy norms of reciprocity" (p. 20). We create each other in community by sharing our talents. Putnam applauds Yogi Berra for his clearly stated definition of reciprocity: "If you don't go to somebody's funeral, they won't come to yours" (p. 20).

How does Putnam explain the collapse of American community? It is not so much that old members have dropped out of community organizations. Rather, it is that community organizations are "no longer continuously revitalized, as they had been in the past, by freshets of new members" (p. 16).

AN AMERICAN DILEMMA

There has always been tension in our society between two forces: collectivism, as represented by community, and individualism. Hedrick Smith (1995) refers to the most dramatic symbol of individualism—the homerun hitter—whose solo performance can "wipe out the opposition with one swift blow" (p. 6). He adds that "it is one of the mindset differences that set America apart from our greatest economic competitors in the new global game" as "the Germans and Japanese, for example, emphasize teamwork over individual heroics, a more gradual scoring over the long term rather than the quick, decisive hit" (p. 6).

A visible sign of this dilemma is found in our schools. Teams and teaming are a major part of the rhetoric surrounding our schools—particularly in elementary and middle schools—and yet we continue to give Teacher of the Year awards. These individual awards are consistent with what Susan Faludi (1999) calls an "ornamental culture . . . constructed around celebrity and image, glamour and entertainment, marketing and consumerism" (p. 35). In short, it is a culture, represented by affiliation, such as the Nike "swoosh" logo, "an affiliation grounded in consumption, not production" (Faludi, 1999, p. 83). *Instant affiliation* through consumption crowds out team loyalty and opportunities for true community. Furthermore, collective learning abilities are placed on the back burner as individual showmanship is emphasized, even though we know that "shared commitment to change develops only with collective capability to build shared aspirations" (Senge, Kleiner, Roberts, Ross, Roth, & Smith, 1999, p. 9).

A conversation with an American teacher or administrator inevitably leads to the matter of parent involvement as a key to creating an effective school. Obstacles to such involvement are many, including overworked parents and family breakdowns. How, then, can school administrators and teachers give leadership to the renewal of the school as a learning community?

THE RENEWAL OF THE SCHOOL AS A LEARNING COMMUNITY

A learning organization is "an organization that is continually expanding its capacity to create its own future."

—Peter Senge (1994, p. 14)

The term *learning community* is often used in current educational literature. A learning community is much like a "setting," defined by Sarason (1972) as "any instance when two or more people come together in new and sustained relationship to achieve common goals" (p. ix). The concept of a relationship is central to the definition, for it suggests an emotional bonding that results from the interaction of persons unified for a particular purpose. In a learning community, the purpose is "learning"; therefore, personal and collective growth are the products of that relationship.

Norris, Barnett, Basom, and Yerkes (2002) reminds us that "community celebrates the dignity and worth of self and others, fosters the empowerment of both, and encourages and supports the maximum development of human potential for the benefit of the common good" (p. 3). Indeed, empowerment is the by-product of a true community, for through unity persons are provided opportunities to realize more fully their human needs, clarify their values, and enhance their capacity for thinking and learning. These three opportunities provide the substructure for personal empowerment.

Creative curriculum leaders are challenged to serve as catalysts for the establishment of learning communities designed to promote this sense of mutual care and responsibility. To care is a matter of disposition and practice. Caring leaders recognize that responsibility to others extends beyond merely establishing good interpersonal relationships with students, staff, and parents. Creative curriculum leaders who foster community recognize that moral and social responsibilities are deeply rooted in the concept of creative leadership. There is a sincere or authentic desire to make a difference in the lives of others. Leaders take on a "servant-leader" perspective that changes the whole nature of the educational process. Sergiovanni (1990) suggests that there is no longer a bureaucratic hierarchy with the leader at the top; instead the organization is based on followership and is guided by ideas, values, and commitments. Leaders become followers and followers become leaders; their roles are constantly changing. Foster (1986) sums up this concept in the following way:

> Leadership, in the final analysis, is the ability of humans to relate deeply to each other in the search for a more perfect union. Leadership is a consensual task, a sharing of ideas and a sharing of responsibilities, where a leader is a leader for the moment only, where the followership exerted must be validated by the consent of the followers, and where leadership lies in the struggles of the community to find meaning for itself. (p. 187)

STEPS AND STAGES IN CREATING LEARNING COMMUNITIES

The first step to be taken is to come together as a faculty and staff to share ideas and feelings associated with previously being part of learning communities at their best. This positive step invokes a hopeful tone to everything that emerges from this point on in the creation of true community. The following characteristics of true learning communities were identified by educators involved in this activity: "I had a sense of belonging or membership." "We listened to what persons had to say." "We publicly complimented and celebrated persons' talents and contributions." "I felt comfortable whenever we were together." "There was respect for diversity and we honored different points of view." "It was OK to make mistakes." "There was a shared sense of vision so that we knew what we were all about."

The second step is the introduction of a model or map that will give participants a sense of direction in the community-building process. The map will let participants know that the leader is familiar with productive ways to move ahead and is not simply "winging it" or flying the plane while it is being built. At the same time, the leader should make it known that the model or map presented is a starting place or springboard that invites improvement as the learning setting evolves.

M. Scott Peck (1987) has created a promising framework with four stages of community building: (a) pseudocommunity, (b) chaos, (c) emptiness, and (d) true community.

Pseudocommunity is the stage during which leaders try to create instant community by using civilities to avoid conflict and individual differences. It is a time when generalizations and platitudes about things held in common prevail. The patter of the cruise ship social director serves as an example: "Welcome aboard to your home away from home and an adventure of a lifetime . . ." Anyone who has been to an "Earth Party" recalls the spirit of the gathering. Everyone on earth has been invited, and hugs are the order of the day. Pseudocommunity is the first stage of community building. An example of this is the setting created by the accreditation team leader who knows there is little time to deal with differences, and many tasks must be performed quickly. Reports must be written, and efficiency rather than effectiveness is paramount. School principals who feel that parent participation gets inthe way of effective teaching and learning involve parents in school rituals that make them feel good without actually participating in the decision-making life of the school.

Chaos, the second stage, occurs when individual differences emerge. Dissonant voices surface, and leaders must reckon with them. Peck (1987) believes that "chaos always centers around well-intentioned but misguided attempts to heal and convert" (p. 90). Leaders want things to be *normal* as various constituencies fight to control the agenda. A superintendent of schools with a good sense of humor entered into a parent-sponsored carnival designed to raise money and create community. He wasn't bothered when a parent pushed his face into a cream pie for a $25 donation to the school fund, but the principal of the school immediately apologized and closed this booth in an effort to return to normalcy. During the first planning session for a "systemwide curriculum audit," an articulate committee member said, "There is no need for this committee to meet as our schools have in place an ongoing system for assessing curriculum." The committee chair, an assistant superintendent, aware of the fact that the newly appointed superintendent of schools, had hung his hat on a curriculum audit, simply ignored the critic and moved ahead with the meeting. The sheer noisiness of chaos becomes too much for many leaders, who quickly invoke an authoritarian leadership style to get things under control.

Emptiness is the third stage of community making. It is the most difficult stage in creating community and yet is essential as "the bridge between chaos and community" (Peck, 1987, p. 95). When asked what is meant by emptiness, Peck (1987) simply says that members of a group "need to empty themselves of barriers to communication" (p. 95). What does Peck mean by barriers to communication? He lists five: (1) Expectations and Preconceptions; (2) Prejudices; (3) Ideology, Theology, and Solutions; (4) the Need to Heal, Convert, Fix, or Solve; and (5) the Need to Control.

This stage of community making was realized during the final class period of the semester of a university seminar. Students were nervous about their papers, which were to be handed in that night. Beneath this nervousness was the issue of grades and grading. A two-hour discussion ensued during which students and their professor emptied themselves of ideas, feelings, and basic assumptions about the reality of the situation. The five barriers to communication listed in the preceding paragraph were overcome by the end of the emotion-filled session. After sharing expressions of pain, suffering, and brokenness, participants seemed to enter a quiet place. It was at this point that the class entered the final stage of community making—true community.

True community is a rare mix of time and place. Once community members achieve this state, they decide where to go from there. If the community is task oriented and involved in problem solving, it can move ahead with its original goal in mind. This occurred at a dissertation seminar. Students spent the first two-thirds of the semester working their way through the three earlier stages of community-building. During the last third of the seminar, they helped each other sharpen their dissertation proposal outlines. If members who have achieved true community are not in a task-oriented setting, they may simply enter into conversation and enjoy each other's company. Peck (1987) cautions us not to think that life in true community is easier or more comfortable, "But it is certainly more *lively,* more intense. The agony is actually greater, but so is the joy" (p. 105). When you experience true community, you simply know it.

Another model or map for community building is the Dixon (1995) Practical Model for Organizational Learning. This model focuses on the role of information as learning communities are created. Perhaps the most important point made by Dixon is that we must go beyond the simple assumption that organizations should give attention to individual members' learning. She argues that organizations must "establish processes for system-level learning" (Dixon, p. 1). Her four-step model may be paraphrased as follows: (1) the generation of information as persons act within and outside of the organization, (2) the integration of such information into the organization, (3) the collective interpretation of this information, and (4) action is taken on the basis of the previous three steps. She reminds us that "every step of the cycle must take the collective into account" (Dixon, p. 1).

It is the matter of collective interpretation that is central to personal and organizational learning. According to Dixon (1995), the following four basic assumptions are central to this matter: (1) all persons must be honestly invited to participate in the generation of information, (2) the egalitarian values of speaking openly without coercion and being respected for this free expression must exist, (3) the size and physical arrangements of the organization must allow for and stimulate interaction between persons and units within the organization, and (4) members of the organization must have and use facilitative processes and skills to participate in discourse.

The skeletal outline of the Dixon model may be useful to the school and school-system leader in creating professional development guidelines that will aid community members in using information in a constructive and creative way. In fact, the Dixon model may be easily translated into a checklist that can be distributed to those interested in creating learning communities.

The third and most popular model or framework for creating learning communities was constructed by Peter Senge and is featured in his 1994 book, *The Fifth Discipline*. This book identifies a set of practices (the five "learning disciplines") for building learning capabilities in organizations. Senge emphasizes the idea that the disciplines represent a lifelong body of study and practice for persons and teams in organizations.

Personal mastery is a discipline that "involves formulating a coherent picture of the results people most desire to gain as individuals (their personal vision), alongside a realistic assessment of the current state of their lives today (their current reality; Senge et al., 1999, p. 32). It is cultivating and dealing effectively with the tension between personal vision and current reality that leads to growth by participating in the learning process. For example, a newly appointed principal was concerned about her ability to speak in large formal settings. She assessed her ability to speak in such settings as average at best (her current reality). At the same time, she aspired to proficiency as a public speaker and was willing to use resources to improve. In fact, it was this very tension that served as the friction that would enable her to move forward to attain her goal.

Mental models are internal pictures of the world dependent on the discipline of reflection and inquiry skills. "By continually reflecting upon, talking about, and reconsidering these internal pictures of the world, people can gain more capability in governing their actions and decisions" (Senge et al., 1999, p. 32).

The point is simply that we do not operate in the world of reality but instead act on the basis of maps in our head—maps of reality as we perceive it. The story is told of two old men walking through a park on a beautiful sunny day. One man said, "This is the best of all possible worlds." His friend responded, "I'm afraid you're right."

It doesn't take a new teacher or assistant principal long to recognize the power of mental models. Most of the interpersonal conflicts that occur in a school day are in fact conflict between different maps of the situation. Two students view a discipline problem on a bus differently, and the assistant principal is challenged to deal with the situation. One teacher may believe that with each child she meets comes the opportunity to create a better world, whereas a colleague acts as if they sent her the wrong children. On and on it goes, but different mental models serve as the catalyst for conversations and decision making.

Shared vision is a collective discipline centering on shared purpose. "People learn to nourish a sense of commitment in a group or organization by developing shared images of the future they seek to create . . . and the principles and guiding practices by which they hope to get there" (Senge et al., 1999, p. 32). It is shared vision that is absolutely essential in true community. When the doctoral students in the dissertation seminar came together in true community, they had the shared vision of helping each other construct the best dissertation proposals they could possibly construct. It often takes a life-threatening situation or crisis to bring together disparate people to have a shared vision.

Team learning depends on constructive interaction of group or community members. "Through techniques like dialogue and skillful discussion, teams transform their collective thinking, learning to mobilize their energies and actions to achieve common goals, and drawing forth an intelligence and ability greater than the sum of individual members' talents" (Senge et al., 1999, p. 32). The strong ego needs of individuals are set aside in the interest of team learning. Credit is given to the team rather than the individual—if the matter of credit even becomes an issue. When team learning occurs, members of the team frequently lose track of time because they are totally absorbed in the learning process. A mental picture of educators involved in developing curriculum materials for a unit of study comes to mind when team learning is mentioned.

Systems thinking emphasizes the perspective of wholeness. "It is a framework for seeing interrelationships rather than things, for seeing patterns of change rather than static 'snap-shots'" (Senge, 1994, p. 68). Scientists, including social scientists, are comfortable with systems thinking, whereas those in the humanities, particularly the arts, tend to think more about the uniqueness of each creation. Senge (1994) speaks to this point by arguing that "systems thinking is a sensibility—for the subtle interconnectedness that gives living systems their unique character" (p. 69). It is my view that systems thinking can be a useful tool that provokes inquiry and learning *if* systems created are viewed as springboards rather than fixed structures.

Creative curriculum leaders are challenged to treat reform efforts as conceptual frameworks that stimulate discussion and revision: What is the key concept that identifies and holds together all of the subconcepts in the curriculum proposal? A child's resiliency, or ability to bounce back from poverty or discrimination, may serve as the key concept. Human and nonhuman resources (their acquisition and distribution on behalf of high-risk children) serve as examples of subconcepts). This example of a conceptual framework or system that serves as a map for an educational reform effort demonstrates that systems thinking may help us organize our thoughts and feelings. It also stimulates team and personal learning as long as the system itself is viewed as a springboard open to revision rather than a final product.

Now that we have discovered the value of models or maps that give us a sense of direction for planning and a framework for assessment of personal and organizational progress, we need to turn to a consideration of adult learners.

CONSIDERING THE NATURE OF ADULT LEARNERS

It is important to give attention to how adults learn and the implications of this for the renewal of the school as a learning community. Students in creative curriculum learning seminars have identified the following points in relation to adult learning. First, adults must get to a high level to give to others— namely students, colleagues, and parents—at a high level (Sarason, 1972). So much emphasis is given to missionary rhetoric about serving others that we often forget that those who give must also get. Appreciation for creative curriculum leadership is one of the best motivators there is. A teacher leader actively involved in curriculum development shared her gratitude for her principal's leadership in powerful words: "We have such a positive work environment at school that if the principal asks me to do anything, I'll do it." An African American assistant principal in the same school spoke about how the principal gave her the gift of understanding: "My personal vision, the reason I went into education, is to be involved in social change. This is what gives me energy. Visiting a classroom isn't enough for me. My principal not only knows this about me but she also supports my vision even though she doesn't feel as strongly about this as I do since I have been marginalized most of my life." This wise assistant principal reminds us that adults learn best when invited to use their talents and explore their interests. Merriam and Caffarella (1991) said it best: "Learning in adulthood is an intensely personal activity" (p. xi).

Second, effective leaders involved in creating learning communities recognize and act on the belief that there is no *one* kind of intelligence but rather there are *many* different kinds of intelligence. Howard Gardner (1983) makes the case for eight distinct intelligences in his classic work *Frames of Mind: The Theory of Multiple Intelligences:* (1) linguistic, (2) logical-mathematical, (3) spatial, (4) bodily kinesthetic, (5) musical, (6) interpersonal, (7) intrapersonal (to know oneself), and (8) naturalist (to discriminate in the natural world).

Many of the standardized tests teachers and administrators have taken to get into universities and university degree programs simply do not honor Gardner's position. The same thing is obviously true for high-stakes tests that schoolchildren take. There is a fundamental tension that today's school and school-system curriculum and instruction leaders face in trying to reconcile accountability measures that promote standardization with developmental needs and interests of students and educators. L. S. Vygotsky (1978) reminds us in *Mind in Society: The Development of Higher Psychological Processes* that personal developmental learning varies from adult learner to adult learner and there is no one set stage for all adults to learn a particular thing.

A third factor that must be recognized with regard to adult learning is that adults must be involved in the construction of knowledge. In other words, they should not be treated as empty vessels to be filled with information that outside experts consider important. Instead, adults who give leadership to the creation of learning communities must own learning by connecting it with frames of reference and experience. An assistant principal speaks to this matter: "Reforms in our school keep people so busy that you can do whatever you want . . . including doing nothing. Superintendents know they are accountable for *introducing* reforms because they probably won't be around when the reform efforts are evaluated. I have learned that really important learning occurs when we own and give voice to ideas that come from our own experiences—particularly experiences that are not especially comfortable and may even involve considerable pain."

Fourth, by sharing with others what they have learned, adults learn at an even deeper level. How often we are reminded that no one profits as much in relation to the learning process as the teacher. When we teach well, we search for meaning, and it is in sharing what we learn with others that meaning is intensified (Merriam & Caffarella, 1991). When one's passion for a subject is integrated with an instructor's best efforts, both teacher and students benefit.

Fifth and finally, adults are challenged to learn in a world that is increasingly complex and fast paced—a world that is rapidly changing "the rules of the game." As one wag said, "For every difficult problem, there is a simple and wrong answer." A major issue that adult learners struggle with concerns how they relate to fads—those ideas and programs that are temporarily fashionable. Adult learners are challenged to use their powers of discernment to separate the wheat from the chaff: "What from the many programs and ideas that others are trying to market *will be* with us ten years from now?" "What from these ideas and programs *should be* with us ten years from now?"

The initial step to be taken in relating to fads is recognizing that fads are a permanent part of the landscape of curriculum reform. The creation and marketing of fads are a very big business indeed. Print and nonprint media serve as a case in point. The personal and organizational cost is best captured in the words of John Dornan, in a 1997 interview: "Last year's panacea is this year's throwaway. It would be laughable if the impact of it wasn't so tragic" (Olson, 1997, p. 8).

We may think of these fads as a parade of programs. What is a parade? It marches by and good order is a major goal. It is short-term—it begins and ends. It should be dramatic—a big and entertaining show with spectators watching rather than participating in its creation. It looks good and is stimulating. And someone has to clean up when the parade is over.

What are your alternatives as adult learners in relating to such programs? You may: (a) be a true believer thinking that the show will make a difference; (b) wave the flag and join in, knowing full well that the show is everything to your leaders— not to you; or (c) don't be obvious about not participating for this, too, will pass.

Given the inevitability of fads, what are the specific steps you may take? You must initially be honest with yourself as to your political needs and your learning needs. If your "bureaucratic superior" has hung his hat on a particular fad as the recognition point for getting his next position, your learning needs may not be your primary focus. That is, your honest critique of the fad may be at odds with your leader's ego investment.

If this kind of political pressure does not exist, you would be wise to involve your staff in researching programs and materials. As a community of adult learners, you can share your findings and address the next question, "Who should be involved in discussing and implementing this curriculum change if we decide to go ahead with it?" Finances are also a real issue. What from among the useful opportunities, hardware, and software can we afford? Attention should be given to the trajectory of the proposed reform: "Are we getting into this reform at the front end so that it will have a fairly long life, or will it soon fade away?" Ask the question, "In whose interest is this proposed reform?" Or, stated another way,

"Who will benefit from the reform? The superintendent? The principal? Teachers? Students? A publishing company? A professional organization? Consultants? Special interest groups? Politicians?" Finally, given your position in the organization, are you *primarily* responsible for introducing curriculum reforms? For implementing curriculum reforms? For assessing curriculum reforms? What are the implications of your answer for how you view yourself and how others will probably view you?

It is in doing your best as an adult learner to balance your learning interests with political realities that you will be totally engaged in the dynamics of creating and maintaining learning communities.

CONCLUSION

Educational leaders in the twenty-first century are challenged by the fact that many persons, young and old, feel disconnected from family, friends, neighbors, and social structures. The collapse of American community begs for revival of community in general and learning communities in particular. The brokenness of community is compounded by an American dilemma or contradiction: community and individualism are forces often at odds with each other.

School and school-system leaders are in a position to make a difference in community making. Your passion for this endeavor sets the tone after which mechanisms must be in place to realize your vision for creating true community. The first step is to have those interested in community building share their experiences as part of learning communities at their best. The positive nature of this enterprise is complemented by a profile of those feelings and ideas associated with being part of a true learning community. The second step is to have models or maps that can be shared with others interested in community making. Three maps were presented in this chapter, each serving as a guide for action and assessment of progress.

A major benefit in giving leadership to the creation of learning communities is that leaders are so focused on collective and personal learning that ego-related problems will be minimized, and the twin pitfalls of boredom and depression will simply be avoided.

Case 18: You Are Considering Entering a Doctoral Program's Learning Community

You have demonstrated your abilities as a teacher leader and school administrator to the satisfaction both of yourself and leaders in your school system. You know that you want to remain a school or school-system administrator for the next ten years. At that time, you can retire and hope to be hired in a tenure-track position as an assistant professor of educational leadership in a doctorate-granting university somewhere in the United States. You hope to capitalize on your successful experience as a public school administrator when you seek the university professorship at age fifty-two. Of course, you want the doctoral degree, but you also want to be part of a learning community that will help you grow as a person and educator.

After surveying doctoral programs across the country, you narrow your options to two universities—a public institution within driving distance of your home and a large, private, distance-education program. You turn to the catalogs of these two doctoral programs and discover interesting information. The Ed.D. in educational leadership in the public institution has a strong cultural studies base and is concerned with issues of educational theory, practice, policy, leadership, curriculum, and administration. Questions of moral concern and the cultural context of education are emphasized. Students have five years in which to complete the program, but students who are focused and keep the momentum finish in three to four years. Written and oral comprehensive exams that link coursework and the dissertation are required. A variety of research methodologies are entertained as students do their dissertations.

The distance-education program also offers the Ed.D. in educational leadership. It is advertised as a two-year program, but most students take three years to complete it. The overarching goal for this doctoral program is to train administrators so that they achieve best practices for enhancing student achievement. "After all, that is what we are after these days," remarks an administrator in the program. The distance-education program is in the process of putting its study areas online so that students will have substantially reduced face-to-face contact time with instructors. Students are in clusters (cohorts), and meeting sites are within driving distance for doctoral students. The program formerly had a staff of part-time professors hired from prominent universities in the nation. These professors were nationally known for their research and writing and were used in the distance-education program's advertising as a way to respond to the criticism that the program's standards were questionable. New staffing procedures are now in place so that nationally recognized scholars are not needed at the cluster sites given current goals for the doctoral program. In fact, administrators and staff are frequently graduates of the distance-education program.

Given your personal and professional goals, which doctoral program will you attend?

1. Enroll in the public university's doctoral program.

2. Enroll in the private university's doctoral program.

3. Spend another semester or year investigating this matter.

Case 18: Rationales for the Alternative Responses

1. Given your two major goals, preparing for a tenure-track position in a doctorate-granting university and being part of a vital learning community, it is wise to enroll in the public university's doctoral program. In the first place, those who interview and hire candidates in a doctorate-granting university will not seriously consider candidates from a distance-education, primarily online university. This is in part because those who interview and hire received their degrees from more traditional doctoral programs. They also are wary of a doctoral program that places less emphasis on research and writing than traditional programs do. Their argument is simply that, to advise doctoral students at the dissertation stage, you have to have considerable expertise in doing research and writing, and you won't get this knowledge in a distance-education, online program. You will experience some community building in the

distance-education program, but the fact that it is going online will greatly diminish face-to-face interaction in the community. The educational leadership doctoral program in this public university is grounded in cultural studies and does not simply have a "how to do it" curriculum. Knowing yourself and engaging in higher-level thinking are the key to success as a leader. You can also save a considerable amount of money in going to a public university in your own state. This is the author's preferred choice given your higher education goals.

2. The distance-education, online curriculum is the wave of the future. You will not have to waste a lot of time and money traveling to seminars, and bad weather will never be a problem. If you are among those who are "the best and the brightest," you will impress those who interview and hire candidates for university positions. The graduates of the distance-education program are in prominent positions in school systems and can help you relocate if you wish to be a school or school-system administrator. If you take the initiative, you can help create a learning community of students who are in your cluster. You will have fewer meetings with fellow students now that study areas are online, but you will have quality time together when you do meet. Furthermore, you can initiate contact with those in your immediate area and create a kind of subcommunity of learners. Also, you can network and create an online community via chat rooms and the like.

3. It is to your advantage to wait a semester or two to gather more information and also see how the distance-education program's move to online instruction works out for its students. With time, you will have a stronger feeling about the correctness of your choice.

Case 19: Interpersonal Skills and Creating Learning Communities

You and a few of your colleagues have been invited to a roundtable discussion at a nearby university on the subject of leadership effectiveness in schools. You find the dialogue between you "on the firing line" and the professors especially interesting.

One professor presents the following view, which especially provokes thought on your part: "Leadership is often defined as getting others to do what you want them to do whether or not they wish to do it. Creative leadership, however, is using your talents to help others discover and use their talents." The professor concludes his comments with a quote from page 22 of *The Lessons of Experience,* by McCall, Lombardo, and Morrison (1988): "In college I used my intellectual skills to get good grades by knowing the right answer. But at work, I found out that knowing the right answer was only 10 percent of the battle. Working with people was the other 90 percent. And we hadn't learned that at school." The professor adds, "Interpersonal skills are of central importance in creating learning communities."

You now have the opportunity to respond to the professor's remarks. What will you say?

1. The professor is right on track.

2. The professor is basically incorrect.

3. The professor's remarks are irrelevant.

Case 19: Rationales for the Alternative Responses

1. Most university classes don't teach students interpersonal skills, and yet it is these face-to-face encounters that make all of the difference in creating learning communities. University professors often treat students as empty vessels to be filled with information. Furthermore, using mandates to force people to obey your commands simply doesn't work in a learning community. Those who receive the mandates don't feel a sense of voice and ownership, and they certainly don't have the chance to practice using their own talents. The professor is right on track.

2. All of this talk about shared decision making, site-based management, and the like is simply rubbish. If you want to get something accomplished, you must simply use the most efficient means at your disposal. Knowing the right answer is the key, and you wouldn't have been named to your position if you didn't know what you were talking about.

3. The professor's remarks are irrelevant because analyzing decision making as we have been doing at this conference is a waste of time. "Wishes don't wash dishes." The only thing that matters is getting the job done as efficiently as possible.

Case 20: Living With the Contradictions of Teacher Leadership

You have played a major leadership role in introducing and maintaining a shared decision-making structure in your school. Six teacher leaders, including yourself, are comfortable and effective in their roles on the school leadership committee.

You notice a disturbing trend in your principal's hiring practices. He has made himself open to the charge of cronyism in hiring his best friend, a former football coaching buddy from a school where they taught together, as his assistant principal. He now wants to bring on board another coaching buddy from the same school as a second assistant principal responsible for curriculum and instruction leadership. What will you, the chair of the teacher leadership committee, do, given your strong reservations about this matter?

1. Make an appointment with the principal and spell out your position and rationale in a one-on-one conference.

2. Make an appointment with the assistant superintendent in charge of personnel and make your views known in a one-on-one conference.

3. Simply keep your thoughts to yourself and go about your business without making your views known to anyone.

Case 20: Rationales for the Alternative Responses

1. This direct approach will make your views known to the person you spend a good deal of time with on a daily basis—the principal. He may disagree with you but he can't fault you for going around him or being duplicitous. This is the author's preferred choice. It still leaves other options open to you if you think they need to be considered.

2. The assistant superintendent in charge of personnel is in a key position to keep the second assistant principal from being hired. The principal obviously has a blind spot on this matter, and it will do little good to talk to him. Ask the assistant superintendent to keep this conversation confidential so that you won't be punished by the principal.

3. You have discovered in dealing with other matters like this that the hiring of the second assistant principal is already a done deal. You will simply cause trouble by making your views known. You will never be sorry for anything you didn't say.

9

Teacher Leaders

The next generation of the teacher as leader debate must break new ground; schools must be conceptualized around leadership frameworks that promote a rethinking of teachers' work.

—N. Cranston (2000, p. 123)

The great teachers fill you up with hope and shower you with a thousand reasons to embrace all aspects of life.

—Pat Conroy (2002, p. 63)

The relationship between teachers as leaders and learning communities, the subject of the previous chapter, is obvious: Learning communities provide fertile ground for the development of teacher leadership, and a major part of teacher leadership is creative curriculum leadership. Cinde Rinn (2003), a scholar who has surveyed research and writing on teacher leadership, supports Crowther's observation that teacher leadership remains "conceptually undeveloped and poorly represented in the leadership literature" (1996, p. 305). Rinn also notes that teacher leadership has become synonymous with the drive toward greater development of teacher professionalism. "Professional leadership roles allow teacher leaders to assume greater informal and formal responsibility as lead teachers, mentors, advisory group leaders, curriculum experts, staff development planners and presenters and school reform advisors." She adds, "In urban areas, teachers have exerted leadership in innovations through unions and site-based decision models" (p. 1).

This chapter is written for teacher leaders and those who give leadership to teacher leaders: assistant principals, principals, and central-office leaders, including superintendents. Much of this information will be new to beginning teacher leaders. Others can use it as a kind of checklist to see how they are doing in their present positions.

Tomorrow's educational leaders have an important advantage that most of today's educational leaders didn't have: They are teachers in schools and school systems that have afforded them opportunities to practice leading. Recent efforts to flatten organizations and involve teachers in shared decision making have given teacher leaders the chance to see if they want to be school administrators and, if so, what kind of school leaders they wish to be as they try to make a difference in the lives of children and adults. In short, we have created *within* school systems and schools an administrator preparation system potentially much more powerful than similar efforts at colleges and universities. Many teachers have experienced leadership over a sustained period of time rather than simply reading about it in textbooks, followed by a brief internship.

This relatively recent phenomenon has its roots in educational reform legislation and implementation, which have demanded that teachers assume leadership roles. Teachers need leadership skills to motivate students and colleagues, communicate with and influence parents, identify and use human and non-human resources, and deal effectively with education issues and challenges. We are moving toward a level of decentralization in many school systems whereby schools take on responsibilities that were formerly the province of central offices: staff development, textbook selection, use of the school day, decisions regarding innovative instructional programs, and a whole range of administrative decisions, such as the scheduling of students, teachers, and budgets.

Creative curriculum leadership is an organizing theme that can be of real value to university and school system leaders as they provide professional development opportunities for teacher leaders who may become tomorrow's assistant principals, principals, and central-office leaders. Subthemes are (a) how to prevent derailment and (b) how to deal with it effectively when it occurs.

GROUNDING FOR TEACHER LEADER DEVELOPMENT

Initially, we must recognize that those who are interested in teacher leader development have a set of beliefs or commitments that serve as a foundation or grounding for more technical strategies and tactics. Therefore, I wish to identify and discuss the basic beliefs that I hold with regard to teacher leader development. These basic beliefs or groundings are often silent assumptions that contribute to success or lack thereof in solving problems and reconciling dilemmas. The challenge is to identify and give voice to these silent assumptions.

First, schools and schooling must be grounded in democratic principles. Engle and Ochoa (1988) spell out some of these principles:

> The most basic value of democracy is respect for the dignity of the individual. The second tenet is the right of individuals and groups to participate in decisions within the society as a whole. A third tenet is the right of all citizens to be informed. Fourth, democracy assumes an open society in the sense that . . . it is never completed. There are no final solutions, no unquestioned answers. Lastly, democracy assumes some independence of the individual from the group. An open society requires that individuals achieve some autonomy from their own group. (pp. 9–10)

The following commitments build on the first and central commitment to democratic principles in schools and school systems. A second commitment is that a teacher leader development program must give attention to both political and spiritual power. As M. Scott Peck has stated so eloquently, "political power is a matter of externals and spiritual power a matter of what is within" (1993, p. 128). If our teacher leaders focus only on the political, they will pay a high price: "Politicians strike me as a lonely crowd, making few deep friendships because almost every relationship is tainted by the calculus of power: How will this help me?" (Smith, 1988, p. 92). (The reader will recall that one of the major causes of leader derailment is the self-serving school or school system administrator who leaves others with the impression that his or her personal advancement is the only thing that matters.) The teacher leader or school administrator who is strictly political locates power outside of self. Gloria Steinem (1992) describes this matter: "Hierarchies try to convince us that all power and well-being come from the outside, that our self-esteem depends on obedience and measuring up to their requirements" (pp. 33–34).

This political orientation is realized in a top-down governance style, a bureaucratic model for governance: (a) anticipate public reaction, (b) make the decision, and (c) implement the decision. The bureaucrat's foremost responsibility is to represent and promote the interests of his organization. The bureaucrat gets his authority from a legal contract backed by the rights and privileges of his office. The bureaucrat's decisions are governed by disciplined compliance with directives from superiors. The court of last resort for appeal of a decision by a bureaucrat is a higher management. Once again, this leadership style is reactive and locates power in public reaction to the exclusion of what the leader's internal compass has to say.

It should be noted in passing that a professional model for governance follows a very different path: (a) make the decision, (b) implement the decision, and (c) deal with public reaction. The professional is bound by a norm of service and a code of ethics to represent the welfare of his clients. The professional source of authority comes from his technical competence and expertise and knowledge. The professional's decisions are governed by internalized professional standards. The court of last resort for appeal of a decision by a professional is her professional colleagues.

All of this is my way of saying that the teacher leader as a creative curriculum leader must recognize the distinction between bureaucratic and professional decision-making frameworks while at the same time attending to his or her moral compass. *These days this can be a mighty struggle, given the realities of government-imposed curriculum mandates and high-stakes testing.*

A third commitment that I hold is that collaborative decisions are not *necessarily* better than noncollaborative ones. Skillful bank robbers Bonnie and Clyde certainly collaborated, but to what end? A friend told me that once while teaching a seventh-grade science lesson, a student brought a muskrat into the classroom. The question was raised, "Is this muskrat male or female?" One student suggested that students vote to determine whether the animal was male or female. Collaboration in this case could simply lead to a sharing of ignorance. Collaboration has many advantages, such as getting persons involved in owning the decision-making process as well as the decisions made, but it does not ensure that a particular decision is good or morally sound.

A fourth commitment is the following: Those involved in professional development efforts for teacher leaders can invite teachers to lead, but it is a serious mistake to force them to do so. We encountered this matter in a school involved in the shared decision-making process. A new teacher came on board, a teacher who had been actively involved as a team leader in Florida. We were delighted that she had joined our team of teachers in this elementary school. In fact, one of the things that got her the job was her rich experience as a team leader in her previous positions in the Florida school. We simply assumed that she would be one of the six team leaders in our shared decision-making project. We said to her, "Judy, we are so glad you are here. We know you will want to be a team leader representing your grade level." She cringed and said, "I burned out in my last school. I was a member of the leadership team, chair of the hospitality committee, and curriculum representative to central office. I want to take some time off from leadership responsibilities to reflect on my teaching." We were of course disappointed but reminded ourselves that she had every right not to be a member of the leadership team. In fact, if we had tried to coerce her to take the position, we would have had a less than effective leadership team member.

It is also the case that a formally designated committee, such as the school leadership team, will sometimes fail to deliver over the course of a fairly long period of time, after which the principal will turn to another committee to do the job. For example, in one school where we worked, the leadership committee turned into a "gripe group" because half of its members refused to think positively. They were experiencing difficult home situations that spilled over into their school lives.

The principal could have micromanaged this advisory group by imposing her will on them. Instead, she turned to the social committee as her governance group, and the school climate improved considerably. Once again, forcing a person or group to do what you want them to do simply doesn't work in the long run.

A fifth commitment is to communication. Most communication in which school and school-system administrators engage is verbal rather than written. Listening and speaking are the major vehicles these administrators use to communicate. Part of this process is the construction of a common language. Language is power, as evidenced by the superintendent who always used the term *measurement* when referring to evaluation or assessment. Soon, principals and others in the system spoke only about measurement, thus leaving the impression that student and faculty progress had to have numbers attached to it.

In another school system where I worked, a shared decision-making program was introduced. A teacher in the system asked what we were going to call it. We hadn't given any thought to this matter and quickly said, "The Stone Street Project." Simply naming this in this way evoked a number of unexpected responses by the faculty: "Here we go again, a principal needs a dissertation topic." "Does this mean that we are going to be treated like guinea pigs?" What's in a name? A good deal, we discovered.

One of the most difficult things for teacher leaders to learn is the role of "bracketing" in the communication process. Bracketing is "the temporary giving up or setting aside of one's own prejudices, frames of reference and desires." (Peck, 1978, p. 128). The true listener uses bracketing to communicate total acceptance of the speaker, the result being that the person speaking will feel less threatened and will make himself or herself more vulnerable by sharing more information.

The sixth commitment is to the learning of all participants in schools and school systems: Learning must be at the center of any teacher leader development program. All participants are teachers and learners; they instruct each other in a variety of ways, usually informal, and in turn learn from each other. Unfortunately, this commitment isn't always voiced in school and school-system public relations pronouncements: "Schools are for children." "Children's learning first." The truth is that, along with children, adults are very much a part of the transactional teaching and learning process. In addition, adults must receive at a high level to give at a high level. Show me a school or a classroom where adults are learning rather than treating children as empty vessels waiting to be filled, and you will see a school or classroom where children are learning a great deal and in the process teaching adult educators.

The six commitments regarding teacher leader development serve as the grounding or foundation for the remainder of this chapter. You, the reader, are encouraged to question, revise, and add to these commitments before proceeding to the next part of this chapter.

THE REALITIES OF THE CONTEXT IN WHICH TEACHERS LEAD

It is relatively easy to talk about teacher leadership as an ideal construct or abstraction that should be introduced and sustained in schools. It is when teacher leadership is considered *in a particular context* that reality sets in, because the specific variables facing teacher leaders come into play. It is these variables that will be discussed in this section of the chapter. It makes sense that most of these variables deal with the relationship between teacher leaders and their principals.

The principal is officially responsible for what happens in the school. We can talk all we want about flattening the organization and shared decision making as desirable alternatives to top-down traditional management systems, and yet we can't eliminate the fact that there is a person *officially* appointed to accept ultimate responsibility for what goes on in the school as a whole. That person is the principal. The buck stops there. If a school leaves the track, the principal is blamed by central-office leaders, including the superintendent.

The superintendent of schools sets the tone for principals and their schools. If the superintendent not only talks about decentralization and collaboration but also lives this philosophy of education, it is more likely that principals will do likewise for educators in their schools. All will depend on the principal's primary leadership style and his or her willingness to share power. In short, teacher leadership is principal dependent, and principal leadership is superintendent dependent.

One of the biggest difficulties we have had with shared decision-making schools occurs when a principal fails to acknowledge that leadership councils are, in reality, advisory and recommending bodies to the principal. These representative groups may use a variety of sources of power, such as expertise, charisma, and succor, but they do not have the positional authority delegated to the principal of the school.

If a principal leaves teacher leaders with the impression that they have the positional authority assigned to the principal, these teacher leaders may feel they have been sold out and that the governance system is a sham when they don't get their way on an important issue.

An example of this occurred one December, a month fraught with difficulties because of the pressures teachers and administrators have at home during the holiday season. Three issues came to a head. The first, and in many ways the most important, concerned the location of the teacher assistants' workroom in an elementary school. At the beginning of this shared decision-making project, the assistants were moved from the stage in the cafeteria to an area in the multipurpose room. This area was partitioned by bulletin boards and wasn't the least bit soundproof. Because the physical educational teacher and others used the multipurpose room for their activities, it was difficult for assistants to do work that required concentration, and the noise that assistants made working machines disturbed classes held in the multipurpose room. As the cold weather approached, the problem was accentuated, for more physical education classes had to be held inside the school.

The second issue concerned the supervision of children on the playground during recess time. Some staff members simply weren't supervising students well, resulting in fights and injuries to students. The dilemma could be stated in the form of a question: How can students receive adequate supervision from some teachers and assistants so that other teachers can have time away from the children during recess?

The cafeteria was the location of the third issue. Once again, some teachers and assistants didn't provide adequate supervision of students. As educators know, when a cafeteria gets out of hand, the noise level is intolerable, food and other objects are thrown, and pushing, shoving, and fighting occur. The same question could be raised about the cafeteria that was raised about the playground: How can students receive adequate supervision from some teachers and assistants so that other teachers can have time away from children during lunch?

The convergence of these three issues within the same time period—the first few weeks in December before vacation for the holidays—is important to keep in mind in our analysis of what happened.

The leadership team, elected by teachers according to grade level, spent some time discussing these matters, but they were not resolved. One of the team leaders said, "I knew that things were building up in the principal's mind and something had to be done. I could see the injured children taken into the nurse's room. I also knew that our leadership team was on record as deciding that we didn't have time to discuss the issue until after the holidays."

The result of all of this was a memorandum from the principal stating that (a) teachers would have to accompany their children on the playground during recess time, (b) teachers would have to eat lunch with their children to supervise their behavior, and (c) the assistants would use the teachers' lounge for their workroom, and the teachers' lounge would be relocated in the multipurpose room formerly occupied by assistants. When some teachers asked about the merit of these decisions, the principal assured them that these decisions were clearly within his jurisdiction, for he was the officially designated leader of the school.

When teachers returned from the holidays, the principal's preholiday dictate was very much on their minds. The leadership team and principal discussed the matter at some length. Both sides of the controversy apologized for mistakes made. One thing was clear, however. Teachers and their representative bodies are advisory, and the principal has *official* responsibility for what goes on in the school.

We can see from the previous examples that teacher leaders need to be able to assess their principal's overall leadership style as well as his or her approach to a particular situation. We have found the following Vroom-Yetton (1973) leadership style framework especially helpful in meeting this challenge. (Modification of this framework is as follows: the term *subordinate* was removed from styles C1, C11, and G11; and G111 was introduced as a leadership style, although it was not used by Vroom and Yetton.)

A1 You solve the problem or make the decision yourself, using information available to you at the time.

A11 You obtain the necessary information from your subordinates, then decide the solution to the problem yourself. You may or may not tell your subordinates what the problem is in getting the information from them. The role played by your subordinates in making the decision is clearly providing the necessary information to you, rather than generating or evaluating alternative solutions.

C1 You share the problem with the relevant persons individually, getting their ideas and suggestions without bringing them together as a group. Then you make the decision, which may or may not reflect their influence.

C11 You share the problem with the group, obtaining their collective ideas and suggestions. Then you make the decision, which may or may not reflect their influence.

G11 You "suspend" your positional authority in dealing with the issue at hand and adopt a collegial relationship with other participants. You have the right to argue your opinions in the same way that your colleagues have this right. After weighing various alternatives, members of the group try to implement the position that is most highly favored and generally agreed on as the best alternative.

G111 You share the problem with the group. Together you generate and evaluate alternatives and attempt to reach agreement (consensus) on a solution. Your role is much like that of a chairperson. You do not try to influence the group to adopt "your" solution, and you are willing to accept and implement any solution that has the support of the entire group. (p. 12)

Most principals vary their leadership style according to the particular situation in which they find themselves. For example, if a child is hit by a car in the street in front of the school, the principal will probably use an A1 style. If, on the other hand, the principal has little expertise in constructing a class schedule in a high school, he or she may turn this task over to the teachers' advisory council and operate at the G111 level.

The Vroom-Yetton model is a self-assessment tool that can help you, the teacher leader, make sense out of your overall leadership style as well as the particular leadership style you adopt in a particular situation. This framework can be especially useful when a leadership team and the principal meet at the beginning of the school year. They list examples of the kinds of decisions that fall into various levels of the Vroom-Yetton model. This results in fewer surprises when they face decisions throughout the year. On occasion, a leadership team will invite an outsider into its meetings to identify and discuss leadership styles used during the meeting. This use of an outsider is especially helpful when leaders are so close to an emotional decision that they find it hard to be objective.

On occasion, we meet a principal who uses teacher leader advisory groups as scapegoats for what parents and others consider to be bad decisions made by the principal. This is a misuse of shared decision making, teacher leaders resent it, and the principal's credibility among teachers quickly erodes.

Thus far in this section of the chapter, I have focused on the relationship between teacher leaders and their principal. *Consultants often play a key role in shared decision-making governance systems, thereby creating both opportunities and challenges.* Initially, we must note that there are two kinds of consultants: (1) internal consultants from central office and (2) external consultants from outside of the school system. Perhaps the most important question is, "Did your school initiate contact and ask for the consultant or was the consultant assigned to you?" Ideally, one or more leaders in your school identified a need and asked for help in addressing it. It is frequently the case, however, that someone in central office assigns a consultant to your school because of a need they perceive to exist. A director of curriculum and instruction in a fairly large suburban school system takes us backstage on this matter:

> Our superintendent prides himself on his interest in and leadership on behalf of curriculum and instruction. As a result, he and his wife, who works for the state department of instruction, make frequent trips to conventions featuring innovative instructional programs and projects. Central-office consultants in the various areas of the curriculum, such as math, science, social studies, and language arts, gather the most recent literature and send this along with convention advertisements to the superintendent. Sometimes they deliver it in person to make their sales pitch. And it works! Our arts program, for example, had tremendous human and nonhuman resources given to it after our superintendent went to a convention and heard a speech on connoisseurship by Eliot Eisner of Stanford University. Eisner was brought in as a consultant, and we used many of his materials. The arts are usually the first to be cut in this age of high-stakes testing, and our superintendent's interest in Eisner's work made a very positive difference in our school system.

One of the first questions teacher leaders must address is, "What is the relationship between the consultant(s) and the principal?" In the case just described, the principal had no previous knowledge of Eisner or his work. The superintendent also had no special relationship with the consultant. In a few instances, the principal or a central-office leader has a vested interest that complicates matters for teacher leaders. For example, in one system, the superintendent needed a dissertation topic and research project to complete his doctorate at a nearby university. The superintendent used the school and staff of a trusted friend who was a middle school principal to introduce a shared decision-making project. This questionable practice, which usually involves the hiring of the dissertation adviser or a doctoral dissertation committee member as a consultant, has unfortunately been a norm in many departments of educational administration. The pressure is on you, the teacher leader, to deliver positive results regarding this so-called experimental project so that the superintendent (doctoral student) can complete his degree and declare the project a success, thus building his political capital.

It is helpful to you, a teacher leader, to know what the consultant can and can't deliver. Consultants often play the following roles in regard to their expertise:

1. The consultant has the expertise to help the teacher leader in a direct manner. For example, teacher leaders need help knowing more about decision-making styles and contingency theory, and the consultant has and shares this knowledge.

2. The consultant, although not an expert in the area of concern, acts as a broker who connects teacher leaders with a source of help. For example, the consultant is an expert on organizational governance but is not an expert on a subject teacher leaders have identified as important—how teachers and staff relate to parents and others in the community. The consultant, therefore, brings in a person who trains airline flight attendants to conduct a staff development program on "presentation of self to the public."

3. The consultant is not an expert in the area of concern, and limited resources keep the consultant from connecting teacher leaders with a true expert. For example, the consultant wants to bring in an expert on reaching a special group of high-risk students, but the consulting budget is exhausted by early April.

4. The consultant isn't an expert in the area of concern and doesn't know any experts who can deal with the issue. For example, a few children in the school appear to be unreachable and act out their frustration in ways that are detrimental to other high school students in their classes. The consultant and teacher leaders are also frustrated, and, despite their efforts, they don't know where to turn.

It is this fourth situation that is obviously the most difficult for teacher leaders to face. They and their consultants don't feel they can fix the problem despite their efforts. They are instead left with the understanding that there is a difference between problems that can be solved and dilemmas that must be reconciled.

The challenge to teacher leaders with regard to consultants is to be as proactive as possible in deciding if you need help from outside the school and, if so, to get the kind of help *you want*. When you set the stage on this matter, the drama seems to have a life of its own. Once a consultant is on board, teacher leaders, the principal, and the consultant(s) should discuss as honestly as possible what kind of relationship they want to have with each other. As teacher leaders, you should be conscious of the sources of power available to you, such as expertise, charisma, and succor, so that you can influence the direction the leadership team, the principal, and the consultant(s) take in pursuing goals.

There is an issue of special importance to you, the teacher leader, with regard to shared decision-making projects: the dissemination of information, particularly the results of your shared decision-making efforts. Progress reports, news releases, television interviews, and other accounts of events at your school are usually in the hands of administrators and consultants. This model for the dissemination of information is consistent with the bureaucratic model, for those higher up decide (a) if the information should be released; (b) the medium of the release, such as a newsletter, newspaper article, radio, or television; and (c) the manner or tone in which the information is presented. How ironic it is that those closest to the students, the teachers, often have little to say about dissemination of information about those children.

We urge teacher leaders to play an active role in giving leadership to the dissemination process. It will give you invaluable experiences that will position you well in the event that you become administrators, and it will be satisfying to tell the story as you feel it should be told.

THE TEACHER LEADER AND MEETINGS

How many times have you heard educators say that meetings are a waste of time? In the next breath, they expect you to be a productive participant in a meeting where they are the designated leader. They can't have it both ways. The secret is to have meetings when they can be productive and not have them when they are not needed. When a meeting can be productive, it is important to know how to get what you want out of it. In fact, this is the first question the teacher leader must ask: "What is the purpose for this meeting?"

A personal real-life example from my life will illustrate this matter. We were building the foundation for a new house, and I thought it would be useful to talk to a few mortgage lending agencies about finances. After each meeting, I returned to my family with a sense of no direction and no accomplishment. After talking to our builder, I learned the exact language necessary to meet my purpose and used it at a meeting with the CEO of a bank after brief small talk: "What I would like today is preloan approval so that when the house is built, we can be set to get the mortgage." The CEO looked over the application and said, "You have it." His secretary then typed out a letter to that effect, and our family was on track after several days of not even being at the "station."

Many meetings are like my early meetings with lending institution people. In fact, leaders at such meetings sometimes begin the meeting by saying, "What is it that we need to do today?" A well-run meeting begins by having the assigned leader state the purpose for the meeting. The following is an example:

We have forty-five minutes this afternoon for our leadership team meeting. You will note that our agenda is divided into two parts with information items in Part 2. You can read these on your own. Our purpose for this meeting is to discuss the two items in Part 1: (a) ways in which we can get members of our grade-level teams to give us their views on various subjects more effectively and (b) ways in which we, as members of the leadership team, can communicate more effectively with them. I will take notes on our discussion, type and photocopy them, and get them to you tomorrow.

Several messages have been sent to committee members with the leader's brief introduction. First, the leader has done her homework by preparing an agenda. Second, the leader doesn't want to waste members' time by going over information items that can be easily read. Third, the leader, because of her experience in previous meetings, has developed a premeeting ritual in which she visualizes what she wants to happen in the meeting, thus giving her confidence from the moment she enters the meeting room. Fourth, the leader demonstrates that this meeting is important by saying that she will type and distribute notes from the meeting within twenty-four hours.

I have attended numerous leadership team meetings and can quickly identify those leaders who are true professionals. They are artists who know the correct mix of formality and informality. If the group is moving too much toward one pole or the other, the leader takes steps to achieve proper balance. Committee members leave such meetings with the feeling that much has been done and in an enjoyable way.

One of the biggest challenges facing the teacher leader who is expected to facilitate a leadership team meeting is to keep the tone of the meeting from becoming too negative. A committee will occasionally have a person who simply wants to gripe about everything. Oftentimes such persons are not even conscious of their negative influence. If other members of the committee are engaged in work that leads to positive outcomes, the negative person may well be crowded out of his or her funk. At times, however, the assigned leader will need to address the problem directly in a one-on-one situation.

The teacher leader who is effective in leading leadership team meetings actively listens to language the participants use. Language is a kind of "emotional shorthand" that quickly conveys meanings to people. While sitting in on leadership team meetings, I have collected a number of morale-building and morale-breaking phrases.

Morale-Building Phrases

"I'm relating so much better to _____."

"I'm really hopeful about what we can do together."

"I can express my ideas in these meetings without being shot down."

"We cooperate despite our differences."

"We go to each other for suggestions because we know that we're accepted."

"No one person dominates this group."

"When a person in this group takes on an assignment, we know that it will get done."

"When a person from this committee learns something, she brings it back to the group and shares it with all of us."

Morale-Breaking Phrases

"It won't work."

"Too much paperwork."

"It's too late to begin this."

"What's the matter with the way we do it now?"

"The problem is that they are all just too lazy."

"We just don't have the time to do it."

"All those deadlines."

"With this short notice, I don't have any suggestions."

"You'd think someone else would do it."

"They'll never read it anyway."

"I've already got a full load."

"Let's do it some other time."

"It seems to me this is the job of the leader, not us."

"I'm not paid for this."

"Because we don't really make the decision, we're just going through the moves."

I sometimes ask a recorder to write down key emotive terms during a workshop of half a day or so and then have participants tell me what they mean by these terms. The following list represents the results of this exercise (Brubaker & Coble, 1997, pp. 82–84):

Paperwork—A symbol for waste of time, busywork, extra duties, bureaucratic directives and the bureaucracy itself, reluctance of the leader to accept responsibility.

Deadline—A symbol for the authority of the leader, the bureaucratic hierarchy, extra duties, pressure.

Memo or e-mail—A symbol for bureaucratic hierarchy, a well-organized leader who has taken time to remind group members of what has occurred or what will occur; sometimes all are punished for one person's behavior, feeling that some good might have come from the meeting after all.

Activity-oriented, hands-on, manipulative materials—A symbol for educationese, the need someone feels for students to learn directly by manipulating things.

Objectives, goals, rationale—A symbol for boundaries, and the need to organize to strive toward predetermined outcomes.

Individualized instruction—A symbol for more work on the teacher's part.

Textbook—A symbol for the "bible," keeping things as they are (manageable and secure).

Letter or e-mail from downtown—A symbol for "God directed," more paperwork, authority and power of bureaucrats.

We to I—A symbol for the leader's move from democratic "we" to "I" to draw on higher position of authority as disagreement occurs.

Agreement to adjourn—A symbol for one thing that all agree on.

Informal seating arrangements—A symbol for leader's desire to have cooperative, nonhierarchical sharing of ideas.

Use of first names—A symbol for cooperation, collegiality, no hierarchy.

Leader starts meeting on time, stops when appropriate, has previously distributed agenda—A symbol for the value the leader places on time as a resource for participants.

Agenda—A symbol for the value the leader places on time as a resource for participants.

Leader's smiles, relaxed but organized manner—A symbol for the leader's desire to be there, the acceptance of what group members can do.

Leader's choice of a good meeting site—A symbol that the leader has done his or her homework and cares about participants and the meeting.

Leader squarely faces conflict and differences of opinion—A symbol for the leader's desire to be honest about his or her own feelings and consciously choosing the best ways to express these feelings.

THE TEACHER LEADER AS NETWORKER

Meetings tend to be somewhat formal in nature even when a leader is more comfortable with an informal leadership style. Much, if not most, of the teacher leader's effectiveness will depend on his or her networking ability. Networking may be defined as the informal process of actively sharing information and support. Leaders who are comfortable with more auto-cratic hierarchical decision-making frameworks usually fear networking because there are no clear lines of authority and control is not necessarily in the hands of those higher up in the organization.

The electronic revolution in general and the computer revolution in particular are evidence of the growth of net-working. Individuals don't have to go through layer after layer of bureaucracies to get what they want. Everything from clothes to cars can be ordered while sitting at your keyboard. The direct participation of constituents without having to go through their elected representatives, and the widespread influence of television have created revolutionary changes in our political system. In fact, politicians have to run fast to try to catch up with their constituents.

All of these changes can work to the advantage of teacher leaders as they access and use information. Change can be introduced and maintained, and those things the teacher leader wants to conserve can be conserved through effective networking. Shared learning can facilitate a sense of commu-nity in a school or a setting within a school.

The following suggestions are the result of observations I've made in watching teacher leaders and other educators use networking as a vehicle for more effective leadership:

Sometimes just introducing two people to each other will make things happen. A teacher leader related, "I introduced a member of our leadership team to one of my professors at the univer-sity who is an expert in reading education. They started shar-ing resources—ideas and materials—that made their way into our leadership team meetings."

Taking the initiative, acting, not just reacting, can make a difference. A first-year teacher who was asked to join the leadership team shared her feelings about moving from the reactor to the actor role: "I was reluctant to contact people at first, but once I got started in building a network, things began to happen and I gained confidence."

Occasionally drop by for informal conversations with persons in your network. These conversations symbolize your personal interest in the lives of people in your network. It is sometimes useful to share materials to "break the ice." A sense of humor is also appreciated in informal conversations.

Give attention to members of a person's support group. It is easy to walk by such persons. While talking to a person in your network, listen carefully to discover who are key persons in his or her support group. A teacher leader describes how this worked for her: "I used to just walk by a particular administrator's secretary, but when I took time to get to know the secretary, I discovered a good deal about this administrator's leadership style. And I can get a lot of things done through the secretary that help our leadership team." Another teacher leader described how she got furniture for the teachers' lounge: "I used to give a cursory greeting to the receptionist at the furniture store where we buy things for our house. I discovered, much to my surprise, that the receptionist is in fact the store owner's mother, and she is a retired teacher. Over a period of time, I got to know her well, and she agreed to give our school new furniture for the teachers' lounge."

Don't always expect immediate results when you introduce change in your network. The teacher leader will sometimes be surprised to find that the seed of an idea planted earlier will surface at a later date. The network member will usually forget where he or she originally got the idea and will instead introduce the idea as if he or she originated it.

Don't assume that the chemistry of your one-to-one relationships with persons in your network will be the same when a group of such persons gets together. It is natural to assume that your friends will also be friends of each other, and yet we hear of instance after instance of disillusionment when network members discover otherwise. "We just assumed that our spouses would get along," said one teacher leader, "but the four of us just weren't comfortable when we got together."

Because persons are expected to conform to role expectations in more formal settings, don't be shocked when they act somewhat differently in less formal settings or vice versa. "The first time I met our leadership team chair was when she gave a speech at our faculty orientation meeting in the fall. She seemed uptight and formal. I was surprised at how much fun she could be when I got to know her." It is useful to remind ourselves that both persons and settings have personalities.

Give attention to symbols that indicate ways in which networking is effective or ineffective. A teacher leader was happily surprised when a message she sent to a leadership team member on e-mail over the weekend became part of that member's report to the faculty on Monday afternoon.

Give attention to ways that persons invite and fail to invite others to enter or not to enter a network. "We respect her expertise and should invite her to talk to us about the new reading program at our next leadership team meeting," a fellow teacher leader said. "She has enough to do and really isn't that well received," a teacher leader said about a central-office supervisor. Networking gives you access to information about the effectiveness of persons in organizations.

Be aware of the fact that some people will feel that your network contacts invade their territory. Informal relationships often tend to threaten persons who feel comfortable and secure with hierarchical relationships. These people will therefore find your networking threatening. "How can I run this department when the superintendent makes so many decisions on the golf course?" a director of personnel said.

Recognize the fact that some persons in the formal structure will participate in formal decision-making situations even though they know that the real decision making has occurred or will occur in informal networking situations. There are times when people play out their roles in formal situations knowing full well that important decisions are rarely made in such meetings. Recognizing the importance of ritual can keep you from becoming cynical. Also, it is helpful to realize that you will also be on the other end of this at times.

Give attention to the importance of how much information a person is willing to give about network contacts. The more information given, the higher the trust level.

Be aware of the fact that persons with formal positions of authority will still use old informal networks to some extent. A principal in a new school was somewhat surprised to discover that teachers in her former school still called for advice. These teachers also had a hidden agenda: They wanted inside information as to what was going on in the central office.

Recognize that potential conflict between informal networking and "going through channels" exists. Once again, lateral decisions in a network threaten the command-compliance decision making in the bureaucratic hierarchy. Effective teacher leaders will be envied by some bureaucrats who think others don't know their place (Brubaker & Coble, 1982, pp. 83–85).

CONCLUSION

I hope that I have left you, the reader, with the feeling that being a teacher leader is a challenging and rewarding position in the school and school system. In fact, it is the potential and real problems and dilemmas you face that will bring life to your leadership. To be a teacher leader is to have a vision of a better future. It is this hopefulness that is contagious in a school and a school system. You, the teacher leader, can make a real and positive difference in your school and school system.

Case 21: Teacher Transitions From Lone Ranger to Teacher Leader

You have had what by all accounts is a successful teaching career with support from the principals and superintendents you have known. What most people don't know is how you began your teaching career as a Lone Ranger. You chose to teach in the classroom farthest away from your colleagues and the principal's office. After a few years of this isolation, you realized that you were cheating yourself and your students by not being part of a teaching team or teaching community. You therefore volunteered for teacher leader positions and moved to a classroom in the mainstream of the school. At a recent faculty meeting, the principal asked for volunteers to tell the story of their careers to new teachers during the fall orientation session. You are not sure if you should raise your hand and volunteer for this assignment. What will you do?

1. Volunteer to tell your story at the orientation session.

2. Don't volunteer to do this.

3. Delay for a day or two and then make a decision.

Case 21: Rationales for the Alternative Responses

1. Your story can be helpful to new teachers who are establishing their place for the first time. They can profit from hearing about your early mistakes and transition to the position of teacher leader. You may also benefit from telling your story because it is in doing these narratives—particularly in a public forum—that we make sense out of our experiences. If you fail to volunteer to tell your story, you may well be retreating back to your Lone Ranger position.

2. This may take resources of time, energy, and emotion that could be used better in some other places. Your story isn't all that important anyway. In addition, some colleagues may wonder who you think you are to behave as if you are so special.

3. There is no rush to make a decision. Perhaps you will have a better sense of what you should do by sleeping on the matter.

Case 22: Whose Job Is This Anyway?

You are recognized as *the* teacher leader in your school. This is the result of your experience and expertise inside and outside of the classroom. You and other teacher leaders who represent various constituencies in the school have introduced and maintained a strong advisory team. The relationship you and the other teacher leaders have had with three principals has been excellent in large measure because these principals have demonstrated their willingness to work as hard as teacher leaders do. The problem is with the newly appointed principal. He has not taught in any of the grades that your school serves, and so he is like a fish out of water in relating to the curriculum. Additionally, he has not demonstrated any interest in learning what he needs to know in this matter. Perhaps more important, you and other teacher leaders feel as if the new principal expects you to do his work for him. Then, if things go wrong, he tells parents and central-office administrators, including the superintendent, that you, the teacher leaders, are to blame. Other teacher leaders look to you to give leadership in this difficult situation. What will you do?

1. Do nothing.

2. Go directly to the principal with your views of this situation.

3. Take this problem to key central-office administrators who can do something about this situation.

Case 22: Rationales for the Alternative Responses

1. This is a no-win situation. Those who appointed this principal to your school will be defensive and think that you have no business going over the principal's head. The principal will find out if you take any action, and things could be rough for you at school. The best response is simply to wait out this principal and hope he is transferred soon.

2. Going to the principal is the key to handling this situation well. The way you bring the problem to his attention, however, is vital. You have the interpersonal skills to handle this well, or you wouldn't be the leader of the teacher leaders.

3. This option will work if you go to the central-office leaders who have the positional authority to work with the principal so that he changes his ways. Those you go to must have a record of being discreet. Otherwise, word will get out, and you will be punished.

Case 23: Dealing With a Negative Teacher Leader

Your teacher leadership team has been effective in guiding the school toward its goals. Members of the leadership team are elected by their constituencies—a method that you supported from the onset. In a recent election, however, a constant complainer was elected by his constituency. Since this time, the teacher leader meetings have been marked by his negative tone. What will you, a teacher leader on the team, do?

1. Do nothing.

2. Talk directly to the constant complainer about the problem.

3. Have the team address this issue at a teacher leader meeting.

Case 23: Rationales for Alternative Responses

1. No matter what you do, you will stir up a hornets' nest. The constant complainer will spread the word about how he was mistreated if you address him with the issue. If the team deals with this issue at a team leader meeting, he will feel backed into a corner and will probably attack all of you.

2. This is the best way to deal with this situation. It will be a one-on-one situation, and thus the complainer can save face. It is also possible that the constant complainer will explain to you why he complains so much, and this will lead to an understanding between the two of you and possible improvement on his part.

3. If the team addresses this matter at a teacher leader meeting, the complainer will know that more than one person finds his behavior unacceptable. There is strength in numbers and the constant complainer will be forced to change his behavior.

Appendix A

A Personal Change and
Conservation Inventory

(My Name) _____

What are the three things about *my leadership* that I highly value and want to conserve?

1. _____

2. _____

3. _____

What are the three things—challenges—about *my leadership* that I want to change?

1. _____

2. _____

3. _____

Appendix B

An Organizational Change and
Conservation Inventory

(Name of Your Organization) _____

What are three things about *your organization* that you highly value and want to conserve?

1. _____

2. _____

3. _____

What are three things about *your organization* that you want to change?

1. _____

2. _____

3. _____

Appendix C

Traits of Outstanding Leaders

After experiencing a situation in which I felt a leader was brilliant, students were asked to tell a story about an experience they had when an administrator or leader was brilliant or superior. We then listed the qualities of the leader at that time. Please use the following as a checklist to characterize a leader who was brilliant or superior in a situation you've experienced:

1. Used applied intelligence (high-level common sense). _____

2. Was authoritative (had a sense of presence). _____

3. Did his or her homework (facts + frameworks/context). _____

4. An expert planner left situation with concrete next steps in mind. _____

5. Sense of purpose (vision) stated clearly and referred to when appropriate. Clearly committed. _____

6. Listened well and spoke to persons at their level. _____

7. Fair. _____

8. Authentic or genuine (not phony). _____

9. Compassionate (not patronizing) and sensitive. _____

10. Not mean-spirited. Has a sense of humor. _____

11. Willing to take risks (to make himself or herself vulnerable). _____

12. Trusts (able to bracket self and look at situation with objectivity). _____

13. Good of the organization a primary consideration. _____

14. Able to build partnerships. _____

Appendix D

*Sources of Power Available to the
Creative Curriculum Leader*

Positional authority

Expertise

Charisma

Succor

Appendix E

Effective Communication

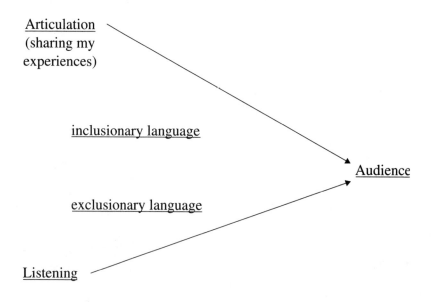

Articulation
(sharing my
experiences)

<u>inclusionary language</u>

<u>exclusionary language</u>

Audience

Listening

<u>selective</u>

<u>true</u> (total attention—role of "bracketing")

Appendix F

The Power of Critique

Critique is the lifeblood of creative curriculum leadership. It is sometimes defined as the art or practice of criticism. Critique can be much more than this deficit definition that focuses on what is wrong or missing, however. Critique occurs when the leader (a) reviews what has taken place, (b) adopts a point of view (thesis) as to what took place, and (c) supports this point of view or thesis. Please give examples of your engagement in critique during a typical workday:

1. _____

2. _____

3. _____

What are some of the subtle dynamics involved in bringing excellence to critique? The first is *discernment*. To discern is to see clearly or differentiate the important from the less important. Making such a judgment always depends on a particular *context*. In other words, one must move beyond generalizations to describe clearly what is happening within a context. For example, Paul is a seventh grader who is called to the principal's office for possessing metallic knuckles. The principal knows that metallic knuckles are considered a weapon—an offense that carries a ten-day out-of-school suspension. The principal is aware that this is a first offense for Paul, as well as the fact that Paul is living with his grandmother because his father is in jail and Paul's alcoholic mother is living with a man who is a drug addict. In fact, Paul got the metallic knuckles from this man. The principal, the school resource officer, Paul, and Paul's grandmother had a lengthy discussion during which Paul was visibly shaken by the gravity of what he had done. The principal, on consultation with the school resource officer, decided to give Paul a three-day in-school suspension with the understanding that a second offense would automatically kick in a ten-day out-of-school suspension.

Please briefly describe situations in which you used discernment within a particular context to reach what you considered to be a fair and reasonable decision.

_____

_____

_____

Appendix G

Reconciling Internal and External Authority

Inner Curriculum and Outer Curriculum

You have recently read *Revolution From Within*, a powerful book by Gloria Steinem (1992). A quote from the book especially stands out in your mind:

Hierarchies try to convince us that all power and well-being come from the outside, that our self-esteem depends on obedience and measuring up to their requirements. (pp. 33–34)

An interview of Steinem by J. Attinger (1992) provides you with another important Steinem quote that catches your attention:

Self-authority is the single most radical idea there is and there is a real hunger for putting the personal and the external back together again. (p. 55)

What is your reaction to these quotes? Do you agree? Disagree? Why?

A day after reading these quotes, you attend a workshop where two representatives from each school in your district listen to a curriculum consultant who states the following:

Welcome to our workshop on curriculum alignment. Let me begin by defining a few important terms:

The Essential Curriculum: the state-mandated curriculum

The Tested Curriculum: the curriculum required for students to perform well on standardized tests mandated by the state

Curriculum Alignment: the proper adjustment of what is taught so that the essential curriculum and the tested curriculum are in line with each other.

The remainder of the workshop demonstrates how essential curriculum materials constructed by the state department of instruction are to be used by teachers.

What is your reaction to this workshop as it is described? Is your position consistent with the position you took in regard to the Steinem quotes?

_____

_____

_____

Appendix H

What Works and Doesn't Work in
Doing Staff Development?

You may do this exercise alone or in a small group. If you are in a small group setting, name (a) a facilitator and (b) a note taker or reporter.

Please *identify* and *place in priority order* three things you've discovered do work well in doing staff development and three things that don't work well in doing staff development. (Priority order refers to strength of response.)

Three Things That Work Well in Doing Staff Development	*Three Things That Don't Work Well in Doing Staff Development*
1.	1.
2.	2.
3.	3.

If you have met in a small group, have each group's note taker or reporter summarize findings from small group deliberations.

Appendix I

*Minimal Criteria for
Proceeding With a Reform Effort*

Seymour B. Sarason, author of *Educational Reform: A Self-Scrutinizing Memoir* (2002), poses a series of questions central to your creative curriculum leadership as you participate in reform efforts.

Sarason introduces his key questions with an overall question: "What are the minimal criteria by which you will decide whether to proceed with a reform effort, or, so to speak, forget it?" He adds, "enthusiasm, a high level of motivation, a laudable desire to rectify or improve an unsatisfactory state of affairs, a vision of what can and should be—these, like love, are not enough, hence the astronomical divorce rate and dispiriting reform failures" (p. 113).

Sarason's key questions follow (pp. 113–114):

1. *"What is distinctively different about the setting in which you seek to effect a change?"* For example, what are the formal and informal power arrangements. What happened in the past in this setting when changes were effected? What is the setting's history with regard to turnover of personnel?

2. *"Do you have criteria and ways to determine the degree to which those who are the objects of change see a need for change?"*

3. *"Have you built into the change process meetings or forums in which you and the participants review and assess what has happened or has been accomplished or not?"*

4. *"Because you know, you certainly should know, that one source of failure of a reform effort is that a person in a key role—such as the principal or superintendent—has decided to leave, what agreement should you seek that gives you a role in selecting a replacement?"*

5. *"Given the above questions, and assuming that you have dealt with them conceptually and realistically, do you have the funding, personnel, and time to do justice to the implications of these questions?"*

Appendix J

*Job Interviewing and the
Creation of Community*

You are being interviewed for a leadership position that you really want. The interviewer says, "Interviewers usually ask, 'What have you done or accomplished in your previous leadership position?' My question is somewhat different: What did you *learn* in your previous position and how did this contribute to the creation of learning communities?"

How will you respond?

_____

_____

_____

Appendix K

Your Reactions to Readers'
Comments on Creative Curriculum Leadership

P lease discuss or write your reactions to the following
comments educators have shared concerning the book
Creative Curriculum Leadership.

"The author uses evocative words to let us know that *curriculum* is somewhat different from what we expected."

"It struck me in reading this book that if you don't agree
with the basic assumptions of others, such as your colleagues at work, you don't listen to them. It is hard to
work to listen to the dissonant voice."

"This book helped me see the importance of *voice* and the
words we use. I was reminded of the politician's prayer:
'Oh Lord, teach me to use words that are gentle and ten-
der for tomorrow I may have to eat them.' "

"The book helped me see that expectations are powerful.
They can be helpful or harmful. They can give us a goal to
pursue which is good *but* they can lead to too much stress.
They can put so much pressure on you that the present
isn't lived."

"*Creative Curriculum Leadership* reminded me that there
are a number of questions that I haven't answered to
my satisfaction. It brought to my attention an important
question: 'What still puzzles me?' I'm glad that I still
have enough 'fire in my belly' to search for the answers."

"This book makes it clear that it is easier to try to control everyone and everything around me than to work on changing myself."

"I was reminded in reading the last chapter that when things go wrong in our school the superintendent doesn't bring in the leadership team. He brings in me—*the principal.*"

References

Adams, J. G. (1983). *Without precedent*. New York: Horton.

Attinger, J. (1992, March 9). Steinem: Tying politics to the personal. *Time*, p. 55.

Austin, G. (1993). Conversation with the author.

Austin, G., & Brubaker, D. (1988). Making the right calls. *Piedmont Airlines, 15*, pp. 103–105.

Bly, R. (1990). *Iron John*. Reading, MA: Addison-Wesley.

Bogdan, R. L., & Biklen, S. (1982). *Qualitative research for education*. Boston: Allyn & Bacon.

Bogen, J. (1979). Some educational aspects of hemispheric specialization. *Dromenon, 1*, 16–21.

Brislin, R. W., Cushner, K., Cherrie, C., & Yong, M. (1986). *Intercultural interactions*. Beverly Hills, CA: Sage.

Brubaker, D. (1967). *Alternative directions for the social studies*. Scranton, PA: International Textbook.

Brubaker, D. (1979). *Who's teaching—who's learning?* Santa Monica, CA: Goodyear.

Brubaker, D. (1982a). *Curriculum planning: The dynamics of theory and practice*. Glenview, IL: Scott, Foresman.

Brubaker, D. (1982b). The underpinnings of creative leadership. *National Forum of Educational Administration and Supervision Journal, 9*, 4–11.

Brubaker, D. (1986, August 3). There's no substitute for wanting to be there. *Greensboro News & Record*, p. E3.

Brubaker, D. (1988, October 8). Leadership: Antidote to boredom, cynicism. *The Salisbury Post*, p. 8.

Brubaker, D. (1989). A curriculum leader's search for meaning. *Journal of Instructional Psychology, 16*, 107–111.

Brubaker, D., & Coble, L. D. (1997). *Staying on track*. Thousand Oaks, CA: Corwin.

Brubaker, D., & Kinard, L. (1988, July 10). Let the "fire" inside express itself. *Greensboro News & Record*, p. E3.

Brubaker, D., & Nelson, R. (1974). *Creative survival in educational bureaucracies*. Berkeley, CA: McCutchan.

Brubaker, D., & Simon, L. (1993). *Teacher as decision-maker*. Newbury Park, CA: Corwin.

Buber, M. (1970). *I and thou*. New York: Scribner.

Buckley, W. (1976). *Airborne*. Boston: Little, Brown.

Buckley, W. (1982). *Atlantic high*. Boston: Little, Brown.

Callahan, S. (1986). *Adrift*. New York: Ballantine.

Combs, A., Avila, D., & Purkey, W. (1971). *Helping relationships*. Boston: Allyn & Bacon.

Conroy, P. (2002). *My losing season*. Garden City, NJ: Doubleday.

Covey, S. (1989). *The 7 habits of highly effective people*. New York: Simon & Schuster.

Cranston, N. (2000). Teachers as leaders: A critical agenda for the new millennium. *Asia-Pacific Journal of Teacher Education, 28,* 123–132.

Crowther, F. (1996). Teacher leadership: Exploration in theory and practice. *Leading and Managing, 2,* 304–321.

Deford, F. (1992, April 20). Arthur Ashe's secret. *Newsweek*, pp. 62–63.

Dixon, N. (1995). *A practical model for organizational learning*. Greensboro, NC: Center for Creative Leadership Issues and Observations.

Dreyfuss, R. (1986, March 23). Interview. *Parade Magazine*, pp. 6–7.

DuVall, L. (1989, February 4). Speech to graduate students in Educational Administration, Higher Education and Research, University of North Carolina at Greensboro.

Eisner, E. W. (1988). The primacy of experience and the politics of method. *Educational Researcher, 17,* 15–20.

Emerson, R. W. (1903). *Essays on history, nature, addresses and lectures*. Boston: Beacon.

Engle, S., & Ochoa, A. (1988). *Education for democratic citizenship*. New York: Teachers College Press.

Faludi, S. (1999). *Stiffed*. New York: William Morrow.

Foster, W. (1986). *Paradigms and promises*. Buffalo, NY: Prometheus.

Fox, M. (1983). *Original blessing*. Santa Fe, NM: Bear.

Fried, R. (2001). *The passionate learner:* A practical guide, 2nd Ed. Boston: Beacon.

Fried, R. (1996). *The passionate teacher:* How Teachers and parents can help children reclaim the joy of discovery. Boston: Beacon.

Fullan, M. (2001). *Leading in a culture of change*. San Francisco: Jossey-Bass.

Gardner, H. (1983). *Frames of mind: The theory of multiple intelligences*. New York: Basic.

Gerth, H., & Mills, C. W. (1946). *From Max Weber: Essays in sociology*. New York: Oxford.

Gibran, K. (1923). *The prophet*. New York: Knopf.

Goffman, E. (1959). *The presentation of self in everyday life.* New York: Doubleday Anchor.

Greene, M. (1975). Curriculum and consciousness. In W. Piner (Ed.), *Curriculum theorizing: The reconceptualists* (pp. 299–317). Berkeley, CA: McCutchan.

Habermas, J. (1971). *Knowledge and human interests.* Boston: Beacon.

Hanifan, L. J. (1920). *The community center.* Boston: Silver Burdett.

Hedrick, D. (1993, June 29). The interview. Unpublished paper. Greensboro: University of North Carolina.

Hutschnecker, A. (1974). *The drive for power.* New York: Evans.

Jackson, P. (1986). *The practice of teaching.* New York: Teachers College Press.

James, W. (1979). *The will to believe.* Cambridge, MA: Harvard University Press. (Original work published in 1897).

Kleinfield, S. (1989). *The hotel.* New York: Simon & Schuster.

Lightfoot, S. (1983). *The good high school.* New York: Basic.

Linver, S. (1978). *Speakeasy.* New York: Summit.

Macdonald, J. B. (1977, December). Interview conducted by Ruth Fairfield at the University of North Carolina at Greensboro.

Macdonald, J. B. (1980). Curriculum theory as intentional activity. *Humanistic Education Project Paper No. 20* (pp. 1–6). Greensboro: University of North Carolina.

May, R. (1972). *Power and innocence.* New York: Norton.

May, R. (1975). *The courage to be.* New York: Bantam.

McCall, M., Lombardo, M., & Morrison, A. (1988). *The lessons of experience.* Lexington, MA: Lexington Books.

Merriam, S. B., & Caffarella, R. S. (1991). *Learning in adulthood.* San Francisco: Jossey-Bass.

Norris, C., Barnett, B., Basom, M., & Yerkes, D. (2002). *Developing educational leaders, a working model: The learning community in action.* New York: Teachers College Press.

Olson, L. (1997, January 22). Keeping tabs on quality. Quality counts: A report on the condition of public education in the 50 states. *Education Week, 16,* 7–17.

Peck, M. S. (1978). *The road less traveled.* New York: Simon & Schuster.

Peck, M. S. (1987). *The different drum.* New York: Simon & Schuster.

Peck, M. S. (1993). *A world waiting to be born: Civility rediscovered.* New York: Bantam.

Pinar, W. (1975). The analysis of educational experience. In W. Pinar (Ed.), *Curriculum theorizing: The reconceptualists* (pp. 384–395). Berkeley, CA: McCutchan.

Putnam, R. D. (2000). *Bowling alone: The collapse and revival of American community.* New York: Simon & Schuster.

Rinn, C. (2003). The artistry of building teacher leadership in K–12 schools: A narrative study of teacher-leaders in North Carolina. Unpublished doctoral dissertation, University of North Carolina at Greensboro.

Sarason, S. (1971). *The culture of the school and the problem of change.* Boston: Allyn & Bacon.

Sarason, S. (1972). *The creation of settings and the future societies.* San Francisco: Jossey-Bass.

Sarason, S. (1993a). *The case for change.* San Francisco: Jossey-Bass.

Sarason, S. (1993b). *Letters to a serious education president.* Newbury Park, CA: Corwin.

Sarason, S. (2002). *Educational reform: A self-scrutinizing memoir.* San Francisco: Jossey-Bass.

Schein, E. (1985). *Organizational culture and leadership.* San Francisco: Jossey-Bass.

Senge, P. M. (1994). *The fifth discipline: The art and practice of the learning organization.* New York: Doubleday.

Senge, P. M., Kleiner, A., Roberts, C., Ross, R., Roth, G., & Smith, B. (1999). *The dance of change.* New York: Currency Doubleday.

Sergiovanni, T. (1990). *Moral leadership.* San Francisco: Jossey-Bass.

Shcharansky, A. (1986, February 24). Visit with a survivor. *Time,* p. 38.

Smith, H. (1988). *The power game.* New York: Random House.

Smith, H. (1995). *Rethinking America.* New York: Random House.

Steinbeck, J. (1952). *East of Eden.* New York: Penguin.

Steinem, G. (1992). *Revolution from within. A book of self-esteem.* Boston: Little, Brown.

Tell, C. (2001, February). Appreciating good teaching. *Educational Leadership, 58,* 6–11.

Tillich, P. (1952). *The courage to be.* New Haven, CT: Yale University Press.

Toffler, A. (1980). *The third wave.* New York: Bantam.

Tyler, R. (1949). *Basic principles of curriculum and instruction.* Chicago: University of Chicago Press.

Vroom, V., & Yetton, P. (1973). *Leadership and decision-making.* Pittsburgh: University of Pittsburgh Press.

Vygotsky, L. S. (1978). *Mind in society: The development of higher psychological processes.* Cambridge, MA: Harvard University Press.

Welsh, P. (1987). *Tales out of school.* New York: Penguin.

Yinger, R. (1978). A study of teacher planning. Description and preactive decision making. (The Institute for Research on Teaching at Michigan State University). *Research Series, 18*(4), 8.

Index

Accountability movement,
xxv-xxvii, xxx, xxxii
Achievement gap, xxvi-xxvii
Aesthetics, 91-96
Affinity connection, 114, 125
African Americans, 138
Amazon River Swim, 76-80
Anxiety:
  assessment tests, xxvii-xxviii
  civil leadership, 114
  curriculum planning, 17
  professional
    autobiography, 40
  vocational nurturance, 61,
    62, 65-66
Artistry:
  creative leadership practice,
    75, 87, 91, 94, 96
  inner curriculum defined,
    22-23
  vocational nurturance, 64
Assessment tests:
  accountability movement,
    xxv-xxvii, xxx, xxxii
  achievement gap, xxvi-xxvii
  anxiety, xxvii-xxviii
  assumptions, xxx-xxxi
  civil leadership, 106-107,
    108-109
  competition, xxvii-xxviii
  creative curriculum
    leadership, xiii,
    xxviii-xxxii

creative leadership practice,
  98-100
curriculum leadership,
  xiii-xiv, xxv-xxviii
district standards, xxvii-xxviii
federal standards,
  xxv-xxvi
inner curriculum
  development, 7, 8
intervention strategies,
  xxviii, xxxi-xxxii
learning disabilities, xxvi
No Child Left Behind Act
  (NCLB) (2001), xxv-xxvi
outer curriculum, xiii-xiv
professionalism,
  xxvii-xxviii, xxxii
racial/ethnic
  differences, xxvi
socioeconomic differences,
  xxvi-xxvii, xxviii
standardized test scores,
  xiii-xiv, xxv-xxviii,
  xxxi-xxxii, 100-102,
  106-107, 108-109,
  138-139, 184
standards alignment, xxvii
state standards, xxv-xxviii,
  xxxi-xxxii, 184
testing irregularities, xxvii,
  100-102, 109
Assumptions:
  assessment tests, xxx-xxxi

creative leadership
  practice, 84
learning communities,
  134-135
teacher leaders, 151
Authenticity:
  civil leadership, 106, 112,
    113, 117, 121
  learning communities, 131
  vocational nurturance, 61
Authority. See Bureaucratic
  governance; External
  authority;
  Positional authority;
  Self-authority
Autonomy:
  creative leadership
    practice, 94
  teacher leaders, 151

Bastian, T. G., 3-9
Boredom:
  learning communities,
    141-142
  vocational nurturance, 57
Bowling Alone (Putnam), 127-128
Bracketing, 111, 154-155
Brislin, R. W., xxii
Brubaker, D., xxi-xxii, 3, 67
Bureaucratic governance:
  civil leadership, 107, 117
  creative leadership practice,
    72, 82, 83, 85, 89-90, 96,
    97, 98
  curriculum leadership,
    xiv-xv
  curriculum planning,
    17-18, 20
  hierarchy dehumanization, xv
  inner curriculum defined,
    23, 24
  inner curriculum
    development, 5

learning communities,
  131, 140
outer curriculum defined,
  20-21, 27-28
professional
  autobiography, 34
teacher leaders, 152-153,
  155-156, 162, 168, 170-171

California Achievement Test
  (C.A.T.), 101
Chaos, 132, 133
Charisma:
  creative leadership practice,
    90, 179
  power sources, 90, 119, 156,
    162, 179
  teacher leaders, 156, 162
Checklist system, 24, 135, 150
Cherrie, C., xxii
Choice makers:
  professional autobiography,
    33-35
  vocational calling, 32
  See also Decision making
Civil leadership:
  affinity connection, 114, 125
  anxiety, 114
  authenticity, 106, 112, 113,
    117, 121
  bracketing, 111
  bureaucratic governance,
    107, 117
  case study (professional
    dress), 123-124
  case study (racist/sexist
    humor), 124-125
  case study (student
    tracking), 118-119
  case study (table manners),
    121-123
  case study (teacher
    assessment), 119-121

charisma, 119
civil rights, 107-108
Commitment
    Scale/Hierarchy,
    106-107, 121
conclusions, 117
democracy, 105, 118
educational goal, 105
energy level, 110, 113
entrance rituals, 110-111
exit rituals, 110, 111
expertise, 119
eye contact, 110
gender-related approach,
    108, 124-125
gifted students, 118-119
honesty, 117, 121
humor, 113, 124-125
inner curriculum
    development, 109-117
integrity, 106, 117, 121
leadership contradiction,
    105-108
leadership contradiction
    reconciliation, 106-107
leadership teams, 122
listening skills, 111
lose-win paradigm, 123
manners/politeness,
    105-108, 120-121
moral behaviors, 105-106
onstage/backstage
    behaviors, 110-111
overview, xx, 68
personal learning, 111, 113
personal vision, 110
positional authority, 119,
    122, 123
power sources, 119, 122, 123
praxis, 117
professionalism, 120,
    122-124, 125
promissory activity, 117

public relations, 120-121
resource conservation,
    119, 120
school metaphors, 108-109
self-authority, 106
self-esteem, 121
socioeconomic
    differences, 119
speaking inventory, 112t
speaking skills, 111-117
standardized test scores,
    106-107, 108-109
succor, 119
table manners, 109-117,
    121-123
table manners defined, 109
telephone guidelines,
    116, 117
television appearance
    guidelines, 114-116
testing irregularities, 109
writing skills, 116
Civil rights, 107-108
Collectivism, 129-130, 134-137,
    141-142
Commitment Scale/Hierarchy,
    106-107, 121
Communication
    barriers, 133-134
Communications role:
    creative curriculum
        leadership, xxix-xxx
    curriculum leadership, xxviii
    effective communication, 180
    See also Listening skills;
        Speaking skills;
        Writing skills
Competition:
    assessment tests, xxvii-xxviii
    creative leadership practice,
        77, 78, 80
    outer curriculum defined,
        27-28

Conceptual knowledge:
  inner curriculum, xiii, xv-xvi
  inner curriculum
    development, 5-6
Consensual leadership:
  learning communities, 131
  teacher leaders, 153-154
Consultants:
  external, 160
  internal, 160
  teacher leaders, 159-162
Contingency theory, 75, 76, 161
Contribution diversity, xxix
Contribution recognition:
  creative curriculum
    leadership, xxix
  vocational enthusiasm, 50
Control theory:
  criticism of, 16
  curriculum planning, 13,
    14-17, 19
  outer curriculum defined,
    20, 22-23
  professional autobiography,
    46-47
Cooperation, 77, 80
Core group, 75, 76
Core self-esteem, xvi, xvii
Core values:
  creative curriculum
    leadership, xv, xvi, xvii,
    xxviii-xxx
  inner curriculum, xvi,
    xvii, xxx
Covenant framework:
  covenant duration, 72
  covenant intensity, 72
  creative leadership practice,
    72-76, 86, 94, 97-98, 100
  high intensity/brief
    duration, 73, 74
  intense/long term, 74, 75,
    76, 100

little intensity/brief
  duration, 72-73, 74
low intensity/long
  term, 73-75
Covey, S., xvi, 76
Creative curriculum
  leadership:
  assessment tests, xiii,
    xxviii-xxxii
  communications role,
    xxix-xxx
  conceptual knowledge,
    xiii, xv-xvi
  contribution diversity, xxix
  contribution
    recognition, xxix
  core self-esteem, xvi, xvii
  core values, xv, xvi, xvii,
    xxviii-xxx
  curriculum development, 1
  curriculum meaning, 1
  curriculum reconciliation,
    1-2, 183-184
  deficit model, xxix
  educational reform
    criteria, 187-188
  experiential knowledge,
    xiii, xv-xvi
  external pressures, xxviii,
    xxx-xxxii
  interpersonal relationships,
    xv, xxviii-xxx, xxxi-xxxii
  leadership contradiction,
    xvii-xviii
  learning activities,
    xxi, 175-191
  learning communities, xxix,
    131, 137, 145, 189
  moral education, xxviii, xxx
  multiple intelligences, xxx
  objectives, xvii-xviii
  organizational change
    inventory, 176

outstanding traits, 177-178
personal change
    inventory, 175
personal learning, 189
political approach, xxx, xxxii
professional autobiography,
    33-38
resource conservation
    inventory, 175, 176
school goals, xxviii-xxix
self-correction, xviii
situational self-esteem,
    xvi, xvii
staff development, 185-186
standardized test scores,
    xxviii, xxxi-xxxii
teacher leaders, 149-151,
    152-153
vocational enthusiasm, 51-54
vocational nurturance, 57-63
win-win situation, xvi
See also Creative leadership
    practice; Inner
    curriculum; Leadership
    contradiction; Teacher
    leaders
Creative Curriculum Leadership
    (Brubaker):
case study design, xxi
case study response, xxi, xxii
critical incidents, xxi
inspiration for, 3
reader response, xxi-xxii,
    190-191
Creative leadership practice:
Amazon River Swim, 76-80
artistry, 75, 87, 91, 94, 96
assumption variability, 84
autonomy, 94
bureaucratic governance,
    72, 82, 83, 85, 89-90,
    96, 97, 98
case study (feminism), 96-98

case study (school history/
    culture), 102-103
case study (shared decision
    making), 98-100
case study (testing
    irregularities), 100-102
charisma, 90, 179
competition, 77, 78, 80
conclusions, 96
contingency theory, 75, 76
cooperation, 77, 80
core group, 75, 76
covenant duration, 72
covenant framework, 72-76,
    86, 94, 97-98, 100
covenant intensity, 72
decision making, 73, 74,
    76-80, 100, 101-102
enjoyment, 80
expertise, 90, 179
external authority, 82, 83
facilitative power, 98-100
feminine approach, 96-98
gender-related approach,
    96-98
high intensity/brief
    duration covenants,
    73, 74
humor, 80
Industrial Age society,
    97, 100
Information Age
    society, 98, 100
initiative, 94
intense/long term covenants,
    74, 75, 76, 100
interaction paradigms,
    76-80, 100, 101-102
interpersonal relationships,
    71-83, 86, 89-91, 92,
    96-100
leadership teams, 75, 76,
    80-82

little intensity/brief
   duration covenants,
   72-73, 74
lose-lose paradigm, 78
lose-win paradigm, 78, 79
low intensity/long term
   covenants, 73-75
masculine approach, 97
organizational vision, 80-83
overview, xx, 68
patience, 80
perception variability, 84, 87
personal vision, 80-83
playfulness, 94-96
political approach, 92
positional authority, 82,
   89-90, 91, 96, 97,
   98-100, 179
power dynamics, 72, 82,
   92-93, 98-100
power sources, 82, 86, 89-91,
   96, 97, 98-100, 179
praxis, 76
priority setting, 81-83, 93-94
proactive leadership,
   82-83, 93
process orientation, 91,
   92-93, 95-96
product orientation, 91-92, 96
professionalism, 96-98,
   100, 103
relationship dependability, 72
relationship evaluation,
   75-76
relationship predictability, 72
resource abundance, 82-83
resource commitment, 82, 102
resource conservation,
   102, 103
resource scarcity, 81, 83, 85
scientific management, 72
self-actualization, 95
self-attention, 93

self-confidence, 78
self-creation, 89
self-management, 80-81
self-understanding, 94
setting aesthetics, 91-96
setting creation, 83-87, 91-96
setting culture, 87-89, 102-103
setting culture defined, 87
setting culture distance,
   88-89
setting culture
   imperatives, 87-88
setting defined, 83
setting history, 83-87,
   102-103
setting history defined, 87
setting language, 88
setting myths, 88, 89
setting reconceptualization,
   92-93
setting rituals, 73-75,
   88, 89, 95
setting symbols, 88, 89
setting zeitgeist, 83-84
shared decision making, 75,
   80-81, 82-83, 98-100
succor, 90, 179
talent recognition, 71-72, 74,
   86, 89-91
talent utilization, 71-72,
   74-75, 86, 89-91
task-oriented settings, 74
teacher leaders, 150
trust, 77, 78, 81, 82-83, 94
vocational nurturance, 59-60
win-lose paradigm, 77,
   78-79, 101-102
win paradigm, 78, 79
win-win/no deal paradigm,
   78, 79, 100
win-win paradigm, 77,
   78, 100
See also Teacher leaders

Creative Survival in Educational Bureaucracies (Brubaker & Nelson), 67
Critical incidents, xxi, 36-37
Critique:
  contextual dependency, 181-182
  decision making, 67-68
  defined, 181
  discernment, 181-182
  power of, 181-182
Culture:
  creative leadership practice, 87-89, 102-103
  cultural distance, 88-89
  cultural imperatives, 87-88
  inner curriculum, 21-24
  organizational, 32
  outer curriculum, 20-21
  setting, 87-89, 102-103
Curiosity, 52
Curriculum alignment:
  defined, 184
  essential curriculum, 184
  external authority, 183-184
  self-authority, 183-184
  tested curriculum, 184
Curriculum audit, 133
Curriculum leadership:
  assessment tests, xiii-xiv, xxv-xxviii
  bureaucratic governance, xiv-xv
  communications role, xxviii
  curriculum defined, xiv, 13
  external pressures, xvii-xviii, xxv-xxviii
  gatekeeper role, xxviii
  political approach, xiv-xv, xvii-xviii
  product vocation, xiv
  standardized test scores, xiii-xiv, xxv-xxviii

See also Creative curriculum leadership
Curriculum planning:
  anxiety, 17
  bureaucratic governance, 17-18, 20
  conceptions of, 13-20
  control theory, 13, 14-17, 19
  control theory criticism, 16
  decision making, 17-18
  evaluation, 14-15
  external authority, 14
  hermeneutic theory, 13, 16-18
  hermeneutic theory criticism, 18
  Industrial Age society, 14-16
  Information Age society, 16
  interpersonal relationships, 17
  leadership contradiction, 17
  lesson plans, 14
  liberation theory, 13, 18-20
  liberation theory criticism, 20
  Management by Objectives (MBO), 15-16
  management essentials, 15
  masculine approach, 14, 22-23
  measurement, 14-15
  networking, 17
  organizational psychology, 19
  personal learning, 17
  political approach, 17
  power dynamics, 18
  praxis, 18-19, 20
  problem solving, 15
  professionalism, 17-18
  reality maps, 13, 14
  scientific-technical approach, 14-17, 18
  self-authority, 14, 17
  self-esteem, 14

task-oriented settings, 15
Tyler rationale, 14-16
Curriculum reconciliation:
    creative curriculum
        leadership, 1-2, 183-184
    inner curriculum
        development, 1-2, 6, 7-9,
        183-184
Cushner, K., xxii
Cynicism:
    vocational enthusiasm, 51
    vocational nurturance, 57

DDB Needham Lifestyle
    Surveys, 127
Decision making:
    choice makers, 32, 33-35
    creative leadership practice,
        73, 74, 76-80, 100, 101-102
    critique, 67-68
    curriculum planning, 17-18
    empowerment, 68
    inner curriculum defined, 23
    inner curriculum
        development, 68
    integrity, 68
    learning communities,
        132, 136
    organizational paradigms, 67
    organizational rules, 67
    organizational vision, 67-68
    paradigms, 67, 76-80, 100,
        101-102
    paradigm shift, 67
    personal vision, 67-68
    possibilities, 67-68
    professional
        autobiography, 36
    reality maps, 68
    teacher leaders, 151, 152-153
    See also Problem solving;
        Shared decision making
Deficit model, xxix, 6

Democracy:
    civil leadership, 105, 118
    teacher leaders, 151
Depression:
    learning communities,
        141-142
    vocational nurturance,
        65-66
Discernment:
    critique, 181-182
    learning communities,
        139-141
Distance-education, 142-144
Doctoral program, 142-144, 161

East of Eden (Steinbeck), 35
Educational reform:
    criteria for, 187-188
    learning communities, 137,
        139, 140-141
    teacher leaders, 149-150
Educational Reform (Sarason),
    187-188
Efficacy-intentionality, 35
Emerson, R. W., 7
Empowerment:
    decision making, 68
    inner curriculum defined, 24
    learning communities,
        130-131
Emptiness, 132, 133-134
Energy level:
    civil leadership, 110, 113
    learning communities, 138
    vocational enthusiasm, 51
Enjoyment:
    creative leadership
        practice, 80
    vocational nurturance, 60,
        61, 62
Entrance rituals, 110-111
"Essay on History"
    (Emerson), 7

Evaluation:
  checklist system, 24, 135, 150
  civil leadership, 119-121
  curriculum planning, 14-15
  inner curriculum
    defined, 23, 24
  outer curriculum
    defined, 26-28
Exit rituals, 110, 111
Expectations, 50-51
Experiential knowledge:
  inner curriculum, xiii, xv-xvi
  inner curriculum
    development, 6-7
Expertise:
  civil leadership, 119
  creative leadership
    practice, 90, 179
  teacher leaders, 156, 161-162,
    172-173
Exploration, 52-54
External authority:
  creative leadership
    practice, 82, 83
  curriculum alignment,
    183-184
  curriculum planning, 14
  inner curriculum
    development, 5-6, 8-9
  outer curriculum
    defined, 20-21
  professional
    autobiography, 37
  teacher leaders, 151-153
  vocational nurturance, 64
  See also Bureaucratic
    governance; Positional
    authority
External consultants, 160
External pressures:
  creative curriculum
    leadership, xxviii,
    xxx-xxxii

curriculum leadership,
  xvii-xviii, xxv-xxviii
Eye contact:
  civil leadership, 110
  vocational enthusiasm, 50
  vocational nurturance, 61

Facilitative power, 98-100
Feminine approach:
  creative leadership practice,
    96-98
  inner curriculum defined,
    22-23
  See also Gender-related
    approach; Masculine
    approach
Fifth Discipline, The (Senge),
  135-137
Focus, 59
Frames of Mind (Gardner), 138
Fried, R., xvi-xvii
Fullan, M., xxviii-xxix

Gardner, H., 138
Gender-related approach:
  civil leadership, 108, 124-125
  creative leadership practice,
    96-98
  curriculum planning, 14
  feminine, 22-23, 96-98
  inner curriculum defined,
    22-23
  male-bonding, 125
  masculine, 14, 22-23, 97
  professional
    autobiography, 36
  school metaphor, 108
  sexism, 124-125
Gifted students, 118-119

Hedrick, D., xvi-xvii
Hermeneutic theory:
  criticism of, 18

curriculum planning,
13, 16-18
inner curriculum defined,
22-23
Hispanic Americans, xxvi
Honesty:
civil leadership, 117, 121
learning communities, 140
Humor:
civil leadership, 113, 124-125
creative leadership
practice, 80
learning communities, 133
teacher leaders, 169
vocational nurturance, 60, 61

Individualism, 129-130, 141
Industrial Age society:
creative leadership practice,
97, 100
curriculum planning, 14-16
Information Age society:
creative leadership practice,
98, 100
curriculum planning, 16
teacher leaders, 168
Information dissemination,
162-163
Initiative:
creative leadership
practice, 94
learning communities, 144
vocational nurturance, 59
Inner curriculum:
conceptual knowledge, xiii,
xv-xvi
core values, xvi, xvii, xxx
creative curriculum
leadership, xvii-xviii, xxx
experiential knowledge, xiii,
xv-xvi
outer curriculum
foundation, xviii

Inner curriculum defined:
bureaucratic governance,
23, 24
case study (curriculum
defined), 25-26
conclusions, 24-25
creative curriculum
leadership, 1, 21-28
decision making, 23
definition, xvii-xviii, 1, 21,
22, 24-25, 29
empowerment, 24
evaluation, 23, 24
feminine approach, 22-23
hermeneutic theory, 22-23
inner curriculum
culture, 21-24
interpersonal relationships, 22
leadership contradiction, 23
learning communities,
22, 23, 24
liberation theory, 22-23
ontological experience, 22
overview, xviii-xix, 2
proactive leadership, 23
right-brain orientation, 23-24
self-authority, 22, 23, 24
service improvement, 24
transformative tradition, 22
Inner curriculum development:
assessment tests, 7, 8
bureaucratic governance, 5
case study (graduate
school), 9-11
civil leadership, 109-117
conceptual knowledge, 5-6
curriculum reconciliation,
1-2, 6, 7-9, 183-184
decision making, 68
deficit model, 6
experiential knowledge, 6-7
external authority, 5-6, 8-9
learning communities, 7

outer curriculum, 5, 7-9
overview, xviii, 1-2
personal experience, 3-9
personal learning, 4, 5-8, 9-11
problem-solving approach, 6
self-authority, 5-6, 7-9
vocational nurturance, 58
Inquiry skills, 135-136
Instant affiliation, 130
Integrity:
civil leadership, 106, 117, 121
decision making, 68
Intentionality, 35
Intercultural Interactions
(Brislin et al.), xxii
Internal consultants, 160
Interpersonal relationships:
curriculum planning, 17
inner curriculum defined, 22
learning communities,
130-131, 144-146
vocational nurturance, 62,
63-66
See also Creative leadership
practice

Knowledge:
conceptual, xiii, xv-xvi
experiential, xiii, xv-xvi
inner curriculum, xiii, xv-xvi

Language:
creative leadership
practice, 88
leadership terminology,
166-167
morale-breaking phrases,
165-166
morale-building phrases, 165
teacher leaders, 154, 165-167
Leadership contradiction:
celebration of, 40, 43, 57-58
civil leadership, 105-108

consternation, 40, 42, 43-44
creative curriculum
leadership, xvii-xviii
curriculum planning, 17
inner curriculum defined, 23
learning communities,
138-139, 146-147
personal, 42
political, 42
professional autobiography,
39-44
reconciliation, 39, 40, 43,
106-107, 138-139
teacher leaders, 160-162,
172-174
vocational nurturance, 57-58,
63-64
Leadership style framework,
158-159
Leadership teams:
civil leadership, 122
creative leadership practice,
75, 76, 80-82
learning communities,
129-130, 146-147
teacher leaders, 153-154,
156-167, 168, 172-174
Leading in a Culture of Change
(Fullan), xxviii-xxix
Learning communities:
adult learners, 137-141
assumptions, 134-135
authenticity, 131
boredom, 141-142
bureaucratic governance,
131, 140
case study (doctoral
program), 142-144
case study (interpersonal
skills), 144-146
case study (leadership
contradiction), 146-147
chaos stage, 132, 133

checklist system, 135
collectivism, 129-130,
    134-137, 141-142
communication barriers,
    133-134
community-building
    models, 134-137, 141
community-building stages,
    132-134
community-building steps,
    131-132, 141
conclusions, 141-142
consensual leadership, 131
creative curriculum
    leadership, xxix, 131,
    137, 145, 189
curriculum audit, 133
decision making, 132, 136
defined, 130
depression, 141-142
distance-education, 142-144
educational reform, 137, 139,
    140-141
empowerment, 130-131
emptiness stage, 132, 133-134
energy level, 138
honesty, 140
humor, 133
individualism, 129-130, 141
initiative, 144
inner curriculum defined,
    22, 23, 24
inner curriculum
    development, 7
inquiry skills, 135-136
instant affiliation, 130
interpersonal relationships,
    130-131, 144-146
knowledge construction, 139
leadership contradiction,
    139, 146-147
leadership contradiction
    reconciliation, 138-139

leadership teams, 129-130
learning disciplines, 135-137
mental models, 135-136
moral responsibility, 131
multiple intelligences,
    138-139
networking, 129, 144
ornamental culture, 129-130
overview, xx, 69
parental involvement,
    130, 132
personal learning, 137, 189
personal mastery, 135
personal vision, 135, 138, 141
political approach, 140-141
positional authority, 133
Practical Model for
    Organizational
    Learning, 134-135
praxis, 135-136
professional
    autobiography, 44
professionalism, 135
program discernment,
    139-141
pseudocommunity stage, 132
racial/ethnic differences, 138
reality maps, 136
reciprocity, 129
revitalization of, 129, 130-131
rituals, 132
servant-leaders, 131
shared decision making,
    145-147
shared vision, 130, 136
site-based management, 145
social capital, 128-129
social disconnection, 127-129
social intercourse, 128-129
speaking skills, 135
standardized test scores,
    138-139
system-level learning, 134

systems thinking, 134, 137
talent recognition, 145
talent utilization, 138, 145
task-oriented settings, 134
teacher leaders, 149-151
team leadership, 146-147
team learning, 136-137, 139
tenure, 142, 143
true community, 131, 132,
    134, 141
vocational nurturance, 63
Learning disabilities:
assessment tests, xxvi
professional
    autobiography, 42
Left-brain orientation, 21
Lessons of Experience, The
    (McCall et al.), 145
Liberation theory:
criticism of, 20
curriculum planning, 13,
    18-20
inner curriculum defined,
    22-23
Linver, S., 112
Listening skills:
civil leadership, 111
effective communication, 180
teacher leaders, 154-155
Lombardo, M., 145

Management by Objectives
    (MBO), 15-16
Masculine approach:
creative leadership
    practice, 97
curriculum planning, 14
inner curriculum defined,
    22-23
See also Feminine approach;
    Gender-related
    approach
McCall, M., 145

Measurement, 14-15, 154
Meetings, 163-167
Mental models, 135-136
Mimetic tradition, 20
Mind in Society (Vygotsky), 139
Moral behaviors, 105-106
Moral responsibility:
learning communities, 131
teacher leaders, 152-153
Morrison, A., 145
Multiple intelligences, 138-139
Myths, 88, 89

Negativity, 164, 165-166, 173-174
Nelson, R., 67
Networking:
curriculum planning, 17
learning
    communities, 129, 144
teacher leaders, 167-171
No Child Left Behind Act
    (NCLB) (2001), xxv-xxvi

Organizational change
    inventory, 176
Organizational culture, 32
Organizational paradigms, 67
Organizational psychology, 19
Organizational rules, 67
Organizational vision:
creative leadership
    practice, 80-83
decision making, 67-68
professional
    autobiography, 35
vocational calling, 32
Ornamental culture, 129-130
Outer curriculum:
assessment tests, xiii-xiv
creative curriculum
    leadership, xviii, xxx
inner curriculum
    development, 5, 7-9

inner curriculum
  springboard, xviii, xxx,
    1, 9, 22, 25, 26
  political approach, xiv-xv,
    xvii-xviii
  vocational nurturance, 58,
    63-64
Outer curriculum defined:
  bureaucratic governance,
    20-21, 27-28
  case study (curriculum
    defined), 25-26
  case study (national
    curriculum), 26-28
  competition, 27-28
  conclusions, 24-25
  control theory, 20, 22-23
  course of study, xiv, xviii,
    xxx, 1, 5, 8, 9, 20-21,
    22-23, 24-25, 26, 29
  creative curriculum
    leadership, 20-21, 24-28
  evaluation, 26-28
  external authority, 20-21
  left-brain orientation, 21
  mimetic tradition, 20
  outer curriculum
    culture, 20-21
  overview, xviii-xix, 2
  personal learning, 21
  professionalism, 21, 28
  reactive leadership, 21
  subject-matter hierarchy, 21

Paradigms:
  creative leadership practice,
    76-80, 100, 101-102
  decision making, 67, 76-80,
    100, 101-102
  lose-lose, 78
  lose-win, 78, 79, 123
  organizational, 67
  win, 78, 79

win-lose, 77, 78-79, 101-102
win-win, 77, 78, 100
win-win/no deal, 78, 79, 100
Paradigm shift, 67
Parental involvement, 130, 132
Passionate Learner, The (Fried),
  xvi-xvii
Passionate Teacher, The (Fried),
  xvi-xvii
Patience, 80
Perception variability:
  creative leadership practice,
    84, 87
  professional autobiography,
    37-38
Personal change inventory, 175
Personal learning:
  civil leadership, 111, 113
  creative curriculum
    leadership, 189
  curriculum planning, 17
  learning communities,
    137, 189
  outer curriculum defined, 21
  professional
    autobiography, 40
  teacher leaders, 155
  vocational enthusiasm, 52-54
Personal mastery, 135
Personal vision:
  civil leadership, 110
  creative leadership practice,
    80-83
  decision making, 67-68
  learning communities, 135,
    138, 141
  teacher leaders, 171
  vocational nurturance, 60
Perspective reciprocity, 38
Playfulness, 94-96
Political approach:
  creative leadership
    practice, 92

curriculum planning, 17
learning communities,
    140-141
teacher leaders, 151-153,
    161, 168
Political contradiction, 42
Positional authority:
    civil leadership, 119, 122, 123
    creative leadership practice,
        82, 89-90, 91, 96, 97,
        98-100, 179
    learning communities, 133
    teacher leaders, 155-159, 173
Power dynamics:
    creative leadership practice,
        72, 82, 92-93, 98-100
    curriculum planning, 18
    professional autobiography,
        34, 35, 37
    teacher leaders, 151-153
    vocational calling, 31, 32
Power sources:
    charisma, 90, 119, 156,
        162, 179
    civil leadership, 119, 122, 123
    creative leadership practice,
        82, 86, 89-91, 96, 97,
        98-100, 179
    expertise, 90, 119, 156,
        161-162, 172-173, 179
    setting history, 86
    shared decision making, 100,
        156, 161-162
    succor, 90, 119, 156, 162, 179
    teacher leaders, 155-159,
        161-162, 172-173
    See also Positional authority
Practical Model for
    Organizational Learning,
    134-135
Praxis:
    civil leadership, 117
    creative leadership practice, 76

curriculum planning,
    18-19, 20
learning communities,
    135-136
Pretension, 61
Priority setting, 81-83, 93-94
Proactive leadership:
    creative leadership practice,
        82-83, 93
    inner curriculum defined, 23
    professional
        autobiography, 40
    teacher leaders, 162
    vocational nurturance, 57-60
Problem solving:
    curriculum planning, 15
    distance from, 62-63
    reflection on, 62-63
    vocational calling, 31
    vocational nurturance,
        62-63, 64
    See also Decision making
Process orientation, 91, 92-93,
    95-96
Product orientation, 91-92, 96
Product vocation, xiv
Professional autobiography:
    anxiety, 40
    bureaucratic governance, 34
    case study (caring-
        caretaking), 45-47
    case study (personal
        disclosure), 44-45
    choice makers, 33-35
    conclusions, 44
    control theory, 46-47
    creative curriculum
        leadership, 33-38
    critical incidents, 36-37
    decision making, 36
    efficacy-intentionality, 35
    external authority, 37
    financial contradiction, 42

free association, 36
gender-related approach, 36
intentionality, 35
leadership contradiction,
    39-44
leadership contradiction
    celebration, 40, 43
leadership contradiction
    consternation, 40, 42,
    43-44
leadership contradiction
    reconciliation, 39, 40, 43
learning communities, 44
learning disabilities, 42
nonvictim attitude, 34
organizational vision, 35
overview, xix, 31
perception variability, 37-38
personal contradiction, 42
personal learning, 40
perspective reciprocity, 38
political contradiction, 42
power dynamics, 34, 35, 37
proactive leadership, 40
professionalism, 47
self-esteem, 36
special education, 47
subjectivity, 37
talent inventory, 38-44
utilization of, 35-38
victim attitude, 34
vocational calling, 33, 38
vocational enthusiasm, 49
Professionalism:
assessment tests,
    xxvii-xxviii, xxxii
civil leadership, 120,
    122-124, 125
creative leadership practice,
    96-98, 100, 103
curriculum planning, 17-18
learning communities, 135
outer curriculum defined,
    21, 28

professional
    autobiography, 47
teacher leaders, 149-151,
    152-153, 164
vocational enthusiasm, 55
vocational nurturance, 64, 66
Promissory activity, 117
Pseudocommunity, 132
Public relations, 120-121
Putnam, R., 127-129

Racial/ethnic differences:
    assessment tests, xxvi
    learning communities, 138
Racism, 124-125
Reactive leadership:
    outer curriculum defined, 21
    teacher leaders, 152
    See also Proactive leadership
Reality maps:
    curriculum planning,
        13, 14
    decision making, 68
    learning communities, 136
Reciprocity, 129
Reconceptualization, 92-93
Reflection. See Praxis
Resources:
    abundance, 82-83
    building of, 62
    civil leadership, 119, 120
    commitment of, 82, 102
    conservation, 102, 103,
        119, 120
    conservation
        inventory, 175, 176
    creative leadership practice,
        81, 82-83, 85, 102, 103
    scarcity, 81, 83, 85, 161
    teacher leaders, 161
    vocational nurturance, 62
Revolution From Within
    (Steinem), xv, 183
Right-brain orientation, 23-24

Rituals:
civil leadership, 110-111
creative leadership practice,
73-75, 88, 89, 95
entrance rituals, 110-111
exit rituals, 110, 111
learning communities, 132
Roper Social and Political
Trends, 127

Sarason, S., 187-188
Scientific management, 72
Scientific-technical approach,
14-17, 18
Self-actualization, 95
Self-attention, 93
Self-authority:
civil leadership, 106
curriculum alignment,
183-184
curriculum planning, 14, 17
inner curriculum defined,
22, 23, 24
inner curriculum
development, 5-6, 7-9
teacher leaders, 152-153
Self-confidence:
creative leadership
practice, 78
vocational nurturance, 60, 61
Self-correction:
creative curriculum
leadership, xviii
problem-anticipating
process, xviii
Self-creation, 89
Self-esteem:
civil leadership, 121
core, xvi, xvii
curriculum planning, 14
professional
autobiography, 36
situational, xvi, xvii
teacher leaders, 152

Self-management, 80-81
Self-understanding, 94
Senge, P., 135-137
Servant-leaders, 131
Service improvement, 24
Setting. See Creative leadership
practice
Seven Habits of Highly Effective
People, The (Covey), xvi, 76
Sexism, 124-125
Shared creativity, 61-62
Shared decision making:
creative leadership
practice, 75, 80-81,
82-83, 98-100
learning communities, 145-147
power sources, 100, 156,
161-162
teacher leaders, 153, 155-163
vocational nurturance, 58-59
Shared vision, 130, 136
Shulman, L., xiii, xiv
Site-based management, 145
Situational self-esteem, xvi, xvii
Social capital, 128-129
Social disconnection, 127-129
Social intercourse, 128-129
Social networks. See
Networking
Socioeconomic differences:
assessment tests, xxvi-xxvii,
xxviii
civil leadership, 119
Speakeasy (Linver), 112
Speaking inventory, 112t
Speaking skills:
civil leadership, 111-117
effective communication, 180
learning communities, 135
teacher leaders, 154
Special education:
professional
autobiography, 47
vocational calling, 30, 31

Spiritual approach,
    151-153
Spontaneity, 61
Staff development, 185-186
Standardized tests. See
    Assessment tests
Steinbeck, J., 35
Steinem, G., xv, 183
Student interaction, 51
Student responsibility, 51
Student tracking, 118-119
Subjectivity, 37
Succor:
    civil leadership, 119
    creative leadership practice,
        90, 179
    teacher leaders, 156, 162
Symbols, 88, 89
System-level learning:
    learning communities, 134
    teacher leaders, 155
Systems thinking, 134, 137

Talent interest, 58-59, 60
Talent inventory:
    professional autobiography,
        38-44
    vocational nurturance, 58-59
Talent proficiency, 58-59
Talent recognition:
    creative leadership practice,
        71-72, 74, 86, 89-91
    learning communities, 145
    vocational nurturance,
        57-58, 62
Talent utilization:
    creative leadership practice,
        71-72, 74-75, 86, 89-91
    learning communities,
        138, 145
    vocational nurturance, 59
Tales out of School (Welsh), 17
Task concentration, 61

Task-oriented settings:
    creative leadership
        practice, 74
    curriculum planning, 15
    learning communities, 134
Teacher leaders:
    assumptions, 151
    autonomy, 151
    bracketing, 154-155
    bureaucratic
        governance, 152-153,
            155-156, 162, 168,
            170-171
    case study (expertise),
        172-173
    case study (lone ranger),
        171-172
    case study (negativity),
        173-174
    charisma, 156, 162
    checklist system, 150
    consensual leadership,
        153-154
    consultants, 159-162
    creative curriculum
        leadership, 149-151,
            152-153
    creative leadership
        practice, 150
    decision making, 151,
        152-153
    democracy, 151
    development beliefs,
        151-155
    educational reform, 149-150
    expertise, 156, 161-162,
        172-173
    external authority, 151-153
    external consultants, 160
    humor, 169
    Information Age society, 168
    information dissemination,
        162-163

internal consultants, 160
language, 154, 165-167
leadership context, 155-163
leadership contradiction,
    160-162, 172-174
leadership style framework,
    158-159
leadership teams, 153-154,
    156-167, 168, 172-174
leadership terminology,
    166-167
learning communities,
    149-151
listening skills, 154-155
meetings, 163-167
morale-breaking phrases,
    165-166
morale-building phrases, 165
moral responsibility, 152-153
negativity, 164, 165-166,
    173-174
networking, 167-171
overview, xx-xxi, 69
personal learning, 155
personal vision, 171
political approach, 151-153,
    161, 168
positional authority,
    155-159, 173
power dynamics, 151-153
power sources, 155-159,
    161-162, 172-173
proactive leadership, 162
professionalism, 149-151,
    152-153, 164
reactive leadership, 152
resource scarcity, 161
self-authority, 152-153
self-esteem, 152
shared decision making, 153,
    155-163
speaking skills, 154
spiritual approach, 151-153

succor, 156, 162
system-level learning, 155
Teacher learning. See Personal
    learning
Team leadership. See
    Leadership teams
Team learning, 136-137, 139
Tell, C., xiii
Tenure, 142, 143
Third Wave, The (Toffler), 15
Time, 113
Toffler, A., 15
Transformative tradition, 22
True community, 131, 132,
    134, 141
Trust, 77, 78, 81, 82-83, 94
Tyler rationale, 14-16

Value systems. See Core values
Vision. See Organizational
    vision; Personal vision
Vocational calling:
    career variability, 30
    choice makers, 32
    conceptions of, 29-32, 33
    destiny, 30
    helpfulness, 30
    inner voice, 33
    love of children, 30
    martyr role, 30-31
    organizational culture, 32
    organizational vision, 32
    power dynamics, 31, 32
    problem solving, 31
    special education, 30, 31
    See also Professional
        autobiography;
        Vocational enthusiasm;
        Vocational nurturance
Vocational enthusiasm:
    case study (parental
        self-contradiction),
        54-55

contribution recognition, 50
creative curriculum
    leadership, 51-54
curiosity, 52
cynicism, 51
energy level, 51
expectations, 50-51
exploration, 52-54
eye contact, 50
overview, xx, 32
personal learning, 52-54
professional
    autobiography, 49
professionalism, 55
student interaction, 51
student responsibility, 51
Vocational influences. See
    Professional
    autobiography
Vocational nurturance:
anxiety, 61, 62, 65-66
artistry, 64
authenticity, 61
awareness of, 62-63
boredom, 57
case study
    (anxiety/depression),
    65-66
case study (teaching
    motivation), 63-64
conclusions, 63
creative curriculum
    leadership, 57-63
creative leadership
    practice, 59-60
cynicism, 57
depression, 65-66
enjoyment, 60, 61, 62
external authority, 64
eye contact, 61
focus, 59
getting started, 61
guidelines, 60-62
humor, 60, 61

initiative, 59
inner curriculum
    development, 58
interpersonal relationships,
    62, 63-66
leadership contradiction,
    57-58, 63-64
leadership contradiction
    celebration, 57-58
learning communities, 63
outer curriculum, 58, 63-64
overview, xx, 32
personal vision, 60
pretension, 61
proactive leadership, 57-60
problem solving distance,
    62-63
problem solving reflection,
    62-63, 64
professionalism, 64, 66
resource building, 62
self-confidence, 60, 61
shared creativity, 61-62
shared decision
    making, 58-59
spontaneity, 61
talent interest, 58-59, 60
talent inventory, 58-59
talent proficiency, 58-59
talent recognition, 57-58, 62
talent utilization, 59
task concentration, 61
Vygotsky, L. S., 139

Welsh, P., 17
Wizard of Oz, xvi
Writing skills, 116

Yale Psycho-Educational
    Clinic, 93
Young, M., xxii

Zeitgeist, 83-84